LIBRARY

This book is to be returned on or above
the last date stamped below. Fines will be
charged for books returned late.

**UNIVERSITY
COLLEGE
CHESTER**

A College of the
University of Liverpool

The complete book of
mini
RUGBY

Don Rutherford
foreword by Will Carling

PARTRIDGE PRESS

LONDON · NEW YORK · TORONTO · SYDNEY · AUCKLAND

TRANSWORLD PUBLISHERS LTD
61-63 Uxbridge Road, London W5 5SA

TRANSWORLD PUBLISHERS (AUSTRALIA) PTY LTD
15-25 Helles Avenue, Moorebank, NSW 2170

TRANSWORLD PUBLISHERS (NZ) LTD
3 William Pickering Drive, Albany, Auckland

Published 1993 by Partridge Press
a division of Transworld Publishers Ltd
Copyright © Don Rutherford 1993

A catalogue record for this book is
available from the British Library.
ISBN 185225 1964

Typeset in 11/13pt Goudy by
Falcon Graphic Art Ltd,
Wallington, Surrey
Printed in Great Britain by Bath Press

Supported by

CONTENTS

THE SUPPORTING CAST

APPENDIX: VARIATIONS ON A THEME

FOREWORD

It is self-evident that rugby is an exciting and challenging game but I can add that it has its own unique camaraderie off the field and this is what makes it such a complete game.

During a match, knowing what you are doing and why you are doing it is crucial for a number of reasons. This knowledge will help you maximize your natural talent, develop a winning style and above all help you to achieve maximum enjoyment.

As Captain of England, I know how helpful Don Rutherford has been to the team with his sound, behind-the-scenes advice and analysis born of many years' experience of the game. This book will undoubtedly get you off to a good start on what I hope will be a life-long interest in rugby. Wearing my other hat as the Honorary President of the Young England Rugby Club, I do hope you will persuade your friends to join our club and keep in touch with England rugby.

WILL CARLING

Note: Throughout the book, readers should read 'he' to mean both 'he' and 'she', and 'man' (as in three- or five- or eight-man scrum) to mean three- or five- or eight-player (i.e., man or woman) scrum.

ACKNOWLEDGEMENTS

Special thanks to a rugby buff and artist, Rod Jordan, for his excellent drawings.

Colin Elsey of Colorsport for 99 per cent of the photographs.

Eileen Power for typing the script.

My wife Sue, who not only produced the section on Warm Up/Cool Down, but has supported myself and rugby for an age.

Finally, to all those who give up their free time to teach/coach/play rugby and ensure that it continues to grow and develop into a World game.

RUGBY: A GAME TO BE ENJOYED

1

THE BACK CLOTH

What do Jeremy Guscott, Jeff Probyn and Ben Clarke of England have in common? One answer is obvious, they are all well-known international players. However, their commonality relies on how and where they learnt to play rugby.

All were introduced to the game at their local club and two of them through an abbreviated version of the fifteen-a-side game, called Mini Rugby. Mini Rugby is a nine-a-side game which has all the ingredients of a full game but played on a smaller pitch, with a smaller ball and for a much shorter period of time. Hence it is classified as a small-sided game. Its big brother or sister is Midi Rugby, a twelve-a-side game which is the essential bridge between Mini and the full fifteen-a-side game.

Since Mini Rugby was introduced in 1970, via the Welsh Rugby Union and ourselves in England, it has grown in popularity, and has spawned many versions to suit the culture and geography of different countries.

In Wales it is now called Dragon Rugby; in Ireland Leprechaun Rugby; in Australia, Walla Rugby; in New Zealand, New Image.

Whatever its title, whatever its differences, wherever it's played, it is a recognition of the fact that to attempt to introduce youngsters to the fifteen-a-side game is simply asking them to perform skills which they are often incapable of doing given their lack of physical and mental maturity and the crowded nature of the pitch (thirty players).

It is important to realize that there has been a swing in the teaching of rugby from State schools to rugby clubs in the United Kingdom and Ireland. It is not my place to explain why this has happened or why some parts/areas of the country have been less affected than others. The fact is the change has happened.

Fortunately one consequence of this evolutionary change was picked up from the outset by the rugby authorities, who have substantially increased indirectly their resources to clubs so that the latter have become the new centres of teaching and coaching. The movement of resources (primarily through the appointment of Youth Development Officers, i.e., YDOs) should not be interpreted as implying that the rugby authorities have done so through choice rather than through necessity. They would have preferred the game to have remained school based and they continue to try to persuade teachers to rekindle the flame. However, living in hope is not a very productive or forward-looking policy and so, faced with reality, it has come to pass that the present and future generations of players, excluding those who continue to be taught in the private sector of education, are increasingly, and probably will continue to be, club trained.

This has brought with it an enormous challenge. Teachers in schools are trained for a minimum of three to four years before they are set loose on your or my child. During this training period they normally receive lectures/practical work on child growth and development, how to teach indoors (the classroom or sports hall) and outdoors (on the games field) – each requiring separate skills.

Contrast this with the club situation. Husband Richard has been persuaded by his wife, Gail, to take their two sons, John, eight, and Simon, ten, down to the local rugby club to give her and their two-year-old daughter Charlotte a Sunday-morning break. Much to Richard's surprise he finds that he is roped in to look after a group which includes his son Simon. His qualifications for this important task revolve round a hasty meander down memory lane to remember what he did in his playing days some ten years ago and what he thinks he has seen recently on the television screen during the Five Nations Championship or the World Cup.

His enthusiasm is beyond doubt, his rugby knowledge so-so, but his teaching ability is highly questionable. All parents would be entitled to ask, 'Would you let your youngster disappear into the mountains without them being in the hands of a thoroughly competent and well-trained instructor?'

If your youngster was being taught how to swim, would you expect the instructor to be properly qualified? Of course you would, so why not for rugby, which is a contact/collision activity?

Now lest you think that all who coach Mini Rugby are not qualified, let me assure you that this is not so. Many are extremely competent and have taken and passed the appropriate Governing Body awards. However, some mistakenly believe that status as a former player is sufficient. Not true. Teaching rugby requires considerable knowledge, teaching skill and a willingness to prepare all sessions thoroughly. The easy way on a Sunday morning is to turn up unprepared, divide a group into two teams, and play a game; unfortunately too many would-be coaches take this easy option. The hard way is to prepare a scheme of work to cover the Under Sevens right up to and including the Under Twelves – that is what youngsters deserve. Having decided the skills that you believe young players need to experience prior to their introduction to the fifteen-a-side game, at probably fourteen or fifteen years of age, the coach then needs to plan each session so that every youngster is thoroughly involved and the activities chosen are appropriate to their ability and experience.

It is very difficult for the non-teacher-trained coach to appreciate that youngsters are not cut-down adults. Children do not have the same vocabulary, same skills nor have they reached the same degree of physical or psychological maturity as adults. It's therefore quite wrong to apply adult standards and adult ambitions to persons who, by any definition, are undeveloped.

Having said all of this, Richard and Gail are *most* welcome and with the right attitude to learning and a willingness to make use of all the support on offer from England's Youth Development Officers, books and videos, they can play an invaluable part in the future development of the game. In truth, they have stepped into a great community activity which can help to shape, develop and enrich their lives and that of their locality by sharing in the family of rugby.

Much of what I have to say goes well beyond the immediate requirements of Mini or Midi Rugby. However, I firmly believe that the knowledge of the parent-coach should be substantially wider than that of the young players. I've always believed you should understand the principles or 'basic truths' of the game and its constituent parts, rather than merely take the role of a child minder or activity organizer.

This book is not a list of practices although there are quite a few. If all you want are practices then I strongly recommend you write to the RFU Shop at Twickenham and purchase a pack of eighty Start Rugby cards – they will give you hours, weeks and months of simple practices. What I would like to think this book does is to prompt you to ask yourself why you are involved in the game, how you would plan the programme and then more intelligently select or devise an appropriate practice to illustrate the particular principle you are seeking to teach. If that happens, even on a small scale, my effort would have been worth while and both players and the game will continue to grow and develop.

2

WHY HAVE YOU VOLUNTEERED?

Whatever your reason(s) consider the following before answering the questions. Throwing a ball into touch or kicking it off the field of play when you've been penalized, running back with the ball and not allowing your opponents to take their free kick, stealing another 5 metres when the referee turns his back to check that opponents have returned the required distance or perhaps committing the most common piece of cheating of all, playing those who are clearly over age in an effort to win a competition. These are the commonest but, sadly, all too frequently committed acts which bring the whole ethos of the game into question.

What is much more important than the formal rules are those which are unwritten, some of which are 'illustrated' in the opening paragraph; these are often extremely difficult to convey on paper but are the very essence of the game of Rugby Football and have been passed down by generations of players since the inception of the game during the first half of the nineteenth century. What I am alluding to is the 'spirit' of the game, not, I would hasten to point out, the liquid variety as so many seem to imagine, but the manner and spirit in which the game is played and which is embodied in fictional works like *Tom Brown's Schooldays*, written by Thomas Hughes who was himself a pupil at Rugby School from 1834 to 1841, *Westward Ho!* by Charles Kingsley, and many others.

Whatever the colour of your political cloth it is an inescapable fact that the public schools of England played an enormous part in the early development of both rugby and soccer. In addition, they were responsible for the following: 'It was in the Public Schools during the second half of the Century (19th) that two basic new theories were developed. The first was that competitive sport especially team games had an ethical basis, and the second was the training in moral behaviour on the playing field was a transferable to the world beyond. This new philosophy was frequently referred to as "muscular Christianity", and was also manifest in the common use of terms and phrases from sport to approve or condemn behaviour on moral grounds.' P.C. McIntosh: *Fair Play: Ethics in Sport and Education*, published by Heinemann, 1979.

For example, most sportsmen and sportswomen would understand the term 'It's not cricket', which implies that some form of cheating is, or has, taken place. Well, Mini Rugby is certainly muscular and physical and even if its only claim to being 'Christian' is because, at club level, it is largely played on the Sunday morning, at least the comparison is not totally lost.

Of course, it is the easiest thing in the world to debunk anyone who gets on his feet and tries to tell you that 'it's only a game' and 'participating is more important than winning!' But it really is. Unless you are a fully fledged professional whose living is dependent on winning, it really is only a game and you do have to go back to school or work on Monday morning.

I can think of no blunter way of stating quite categorically that there is no place for those who cheat, be they teacher/coach or player. In the teaching/coaching of young players those who would 'bend the rules', 'turn a blind eye', or 'use gamesmanship' to defeat opponents are outside the barriers of reasonable behaviour. Whatever phraseology you come

DRESSING ROOM
REMEMBER
We all return to
work or school
on Monday
morning!

up with, whatever cliché you hide behind, there really is no place for cheating. If you play over-age players then all you do is debase the intelligence of, and mislead, the young players in your charge, you create a false environment. You also start them on a path which could end by destroying the very fabric of the game. Both Mini Rugby nine-a-side and Midi Rugby twelve-a-side are hard physical games demanding the highest standard of behaviour and attitude from the teacher and coach. Yes, that's where it begins. If you don't set a good example, if you don't dictate the moral code which differentiates between right and wrong then you are doing your young charges, the game and yourself a great disservice.

Back in September 1936 in the Foreword to *Rugby Football, How to Succeed*, a book published for the National Union of Teachers, the then President of the Rugby Football Union, Mr J.E. Greenwood, said, 'Rugby Football is a game suitable only to those who understand and appreciate the "spirit of the game". By this, it is meant that you must strive to keep fit and play your hardest to win; that you must take the Referee's decisions, however unjust they may seem, without any show of resentment whatever; that you must never take advantage of the Referee by cheating; that you must never bear a grudge against an opponent for hard knocks fairly given, for the game is a hard one; and above all, that you will accept defeat with good grace. If you do not intend to try and play the game according to the spirit of the game, you are wasting your time in reading this book because there is no place in Rugby Football for you.'

The pity is that these simple words have not been engraved on every dressing-room door, because in a highly materialistic and soulless world, they are perhaps more important in this day and age than ever before.

There is no doubt that a number of features of the full fifteen-a-side game lend themselves to malpractice because of the dynamic nature of the game and the close-quarter contact, which is not always visible to the referee or touch-judges. Such opportunities are much less apparent at Mini/Midi level. Fortunately television has been extremely helpful in persuading senior players to resist the temptation to take the law into their own hands and not execute their own retribution. The eye of the camera can often see into the darkest of corners and can now be cited in evidence against miscreants.

Having played the game at the very highest level, I am in no doubt that winning is very important. However, I would still place it as my lowest standard. In other words, the manner in which winning is achieved and the quality of the rugby being played are far more important, especially in the medium and long term. To win with style, with all fifteen players being fully involved, now that really is worth while.

The aims of Mini and Midi Rugby are extremely simple and unpretentious – the major obstacle to its future growth is that some of those otherwise honourable and enthusiastic helpers might do the game a great disservice through their very own, but sometimes misguided, enthusiasm.

Instead of teaching and nurturing skill, they applaud the selfish boy who has a half-stone advantage and trundles the others out of his path on his way to the 'try' (goal) line as though he were in a bowling alley. If only we would give the same applause to the boy who gives a well-timed pass and who instantly sees which direction to run the ball from a breakdown.

There is a well-known saying that 'education should be about lighting fires and not filling jugs'. On a less exalted plain, so should the teaching of Mini and Midi Rugby. You see, effective coaching/teaching is a most dedicated and exacting art.

When you do not know what to do or how to teach a particular technique then the easiest way out is to play a game. Now this would not be too bad an approach if more Mini and Midi coaches played three versus three or four versus four, but to play nine versus nine with scrums on the very first occasion a boy is introduced to the rugby ball is, at best, asking for trouble, or at worst, a guarantee that so many boys will be put off the game for life.

This, and for many other reasons, is why in England we have introduced New Image Rugby, a non-contact game – but more about that later.

Again, the attitude of some Mini Rugby coaches, and I am

talking literally about the minority, has also been brought into question. Why are they helping? Is it really to help the boys and develop the game of Rugby Football or are they frustrated former players on an ego trip trying desperately to live out their own unfulfilled ambitions? Such an approach is often epitomized by the ranting touch-line 'helper' who mouths advice which clearly doubts the parentage of the referee, the opposition and insults the intelligence of the players. Sadly, sometimes the mothers are the worst offenders!

I must say I dislike the coach who refers to the players as being 'their team', if for no other reason than the teacher or coach simply cannot play the game from the sidelines, and the quicker this factor is realized the better. Youngsters learn, like everyone else, from making their own mistakes. Let them get on with it – the important task for the teacher or coach is to create the right atmosphere so that young players will begin at a very early age to understand the ethos or spirit of the game, and begin to acquire the more subtle skills of the game.

It is true that some youngsters will ask, 'When are you going to play a game?' and, of course, it is very easy to give in, but you must take the long-term view and judge what is in their best interest. My answer is simple, give the beginners a game by all means but not the nine versus nine with full scrums and line-outs. For the absolute beginners they must first of all be taught the correct techniques of handling, tackling and other aspects of contact before playing the full nine-a-side game. However, if you remove the contact element and simply play one of the many variations of Touch Rugby, like New Image Rugby, then it is a different matter. Telling young players 'it's a man's game' is not going to give them much confidence and besides it's also a woman's game these days. Such spurious comments are no substitute for teaching the correct techniques as the foundation of future progress.

Assuming that you have introduced tackling properly, bearing in mind the safety factors, then why not play a game of say four versus four with one player from each team acting as a forward in turn? Whether they hook the ball in the 'chicken-scratch' method or with the foot is left to your best judgement, as only you, the coach, can really tell of what they are capable.

If it is true that the full fifteen-a-side game cannot develop any shape or pattern until everyone can run and handle as though the ball were an extension of their hands then, equally, it must be so of Mini and Midi Rugby and there is no secret as to how this is achieved. Provided the correct techniques are taught initially, then the rest comes through diligent practice. Newcomers to rugby tend to pass standing still or whilst running laterally towards the touch-line (see Example 1, below). The simple advice of 'go forward' is a timely reminder that as you teach the technique so you must never lose the opportunity to ram home the principles of the game.

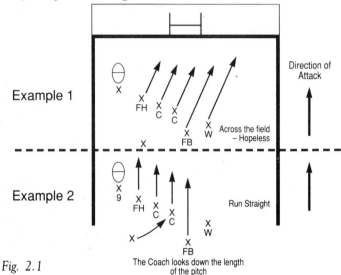

Fig. 2.1

Finally, don't view your opponents as the enemy. Like you, they are taking part in what should be an immensely satisfying social activity. Shake their hands, welcome them to your club or school. Give them a hard game but when it is over thank them and the referee for coming, entertain them and then wish them a safe journey home. Surely that is how you would like to be treated? So why not create a friendly and warm environment, you know it will work to everyone's advantage.

Perhaps you are now in a better position to answer the opening question.

3

THE WINNING WAY

There are all manner of ways of looking at a problem and of coming up with a solution(s). This chapter is an attempt to look at the game in at least two ways, both of which should help you to find a winning formula.

The first is extremely simplistic and deals with four guiding principles; the second way looks at major units and functions. Neither approach is based on some Utopian ideal but on many years' experience as a player, player/coach, teacher and now National Officer. To be a successful teacher or coach you must work from a clear understanding of where you are now, where you want to be in three to five years' time and, especially, how you are going to achieve your goal(s).

3.1 THE FOUR PRINCIPLES

The four principles of the game, which are all interconnected, are 'Go Forward', 'Support', 'Continuity' and 'Pressure'. It is essential that the Mini/Midi Rugby coach should never forget these principles, especially when practising with young players.

There are two simple pieces of advice that those looking after young players would do well to remember.

(1)   Tell them that if the ball is on the ground and it's in front of them they should pick it up and run forward. If the ball is on the ground and it is behind them then they should fall on it and stand up immediately. Now, you and I can think of many situations where this would not be the right decision but, as a rule of thumb, as a piece of simple advice to the newcomer, then I think you will find it works remarkably well.

(2)   As most youngsters won't have a clue as to the markings on a Mini Rugby pitch, at the beginning of a season ask them to run to, say, the opponent's goal line and back; to their own 15-metre drop-out line and back; their own in-goal area and back; the line 7 metres from the kick-off where their opponents will stand to receive the kick-off, and back, etc. Not only will it help them to understand

the geography of the pitch, it will warm them up. Incidentally, if you, as the coach, have taken up a central position, they will have begun to move up and down the field as opposed to across it.

It won't be the first time that I have taken a group of players, sometimes much older than at Mini/Midi Rugby age, on to the pitch and said to them, 'Where is your opponent's try line?' Occasionally they have looked at me as though I have lost my marbles but someone ultimately has always pointed out the right direction. 'Thank you,' I've said. 'Now that you and I both know where the opponent's try line is, do not let me catch anyone running towards the touch-lines!' Again, all I am emphasizing is one of the fundamental principles of Rugby Football – 'Go Forward'.

Ask any top-class hooker what he wants from the rest of his pack and he'll tell you, 'six inches of co-ordinated effort'. That will ensure that he is nearer to the ball than his opposite number and with that sort of advantage the ball will be his. The Mini/Midi scrum is no different as far as the principle is concerned, even though there are only three or five players respectively.

If all players really do understand the importance of going forward then, of course, rarely would there be a need for the unit skill of rucking or mauling when the ball carrier is tackled, because instantly a colleague would be on hand in support and so the ball would continue to be carried forwards towards the opponent's goal line. Whilst this is the aim, breakdowns do occur and rucks and mauls are necessary. Players who arrive at a breakdown bound together and immediately commence driving forward parallel with the touch-line, inevitably win the ball.

Already I have touched on the second of our principles of play, namely 'Support', which was necessary for the hooker to win the ball in the scrum and for the ball to be won in the rucks or mauls. Obviously, our principles are interconnected – none will operate in isolation. Every member of the Mini/Midi Rugby team must support each other in all phases of the game, that is, in attack and defence. The finest back division in the world will be useless, in fact might as well take their boots off and go for a shower, unless the forwards are producing the ball going forward. That means the latter must work and support each other.

No scrum functions effectively unless the weight being exerted by individuals is co-ordinated into a concerted effort and unless binding is iron-tight.

This is the true meaning of support, yet so often people mentally picture support as being a function only of players in the loose. Because the principles of play are interconnected, it follows that if the players are going forward and supporting each other, then they will have a much better chance of keeping the game flowing. In other words, they will give the game its aimed-for 'Continuity'.

Scoring tries is simply a matter of either disorganizing the opposition's defence so that someone is out of position or, in a one-to-one situation, the attacker is skilful enough to beat his opponent by a side-step, swerve, change of pace or hand off. Continuity is only possible if players have been taught how to retain or regain possession.

Players who kick possession away or spill the ball every time they come within hailing distance of an opponent, are luxuries few sides can afford! This principle demands from the player tremendous fitness, quick and reliable handling, and the ability to read and anticipate what the opposition are going to do next, in order that correct decisions are made, which will result in the opposition continuously being attacked at their most vulnerable points.

Sides like New Zealand and Australia have thrived on their ability to win the ball at breakdowns because of their superior support and rucking or mauling technique. The pressure they have been able to exert on weakened and disorganized defences has made them so difficult to beat.

When you apply 'Pressure' successfully to your opponents you reduce their options to zero.

Pressure can be exerted in a variety of ways . . .

(1)   Your opponents might have won their own scrum ball,
        but you exert such drive in the scrum that you slow down
        their heel.

(2)   Your skilful kicking, be it high-hanging, grubber or
        chip, gives your opponents no chance of clearing their
        lines and you catch them in possession of the ball.

(3)   Your tackling is so consuming that they seriously won-
        der whether or not they are playing against a team of
        eighteen opponents instead of nine.

Once you have put the opposition under pressure they will
make mistakes, as sure as night follows day. Your job then is
either to retain or regain possession of the ball . . . Then you
are firmly back in the driving seat.

3.2 THE ROAD MAP APPROACH

I devised the following for the Senior England Team and
supported my beliefs with a video (*The Winning Way*), the
principles are just as applicable to Mini or Midi Rugby as
to the full fifteen-a-side game at all levels. Principles (or
basic truths) do not change . . . with one proviso. If the
law makers so fundamentally change the laws that what was
the accepted doctrine is now unachieveable . . . then clearly
in those circumstances you have to think again. The winner
in rugby is the team that scores most points, not tries, than
its opponents and the formula for winning largely depends on
winning and keeping possession of the ball.

Yes, you must have players with high levels of proficiency
in basic and positional skills, extremely fit players, players
who understand the game and players who have the unerring
facility to make more correct decisions than their opponents.
You as teacher/coach must have a vision of how you want to
play the game, have a road map in your mind which negotiates
all obstacles and – and it's a big 'and' – translate that vision,
implant that road map in the minds of your players.

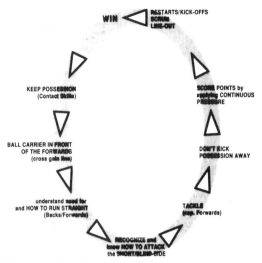

Fig. 3.1: Understanding the game. The winning way.

In an ideal world you would always put the most imaginative, sympathetic and analytical teachers/coaches with the brightest young players. Clearly this is moonshine in most clubs/schools. The reality is finding a willing volunteer. This is what you need to understand and then translate via practical work into player understanding. Your team *must* win primary possession, that is, kick-offs/restarts (including 22 drop-outs), scrums and line-outs. As teacher/coach this is what you look for:

KICK-OFF/RESTARTS (including 15/22 drop-outs)

At the kick-off the first requirement is for accuracy from the kicker. Kicking straight into touch is not only embarrassing but it also gives your opponents the advantage either of accepting the line-out or of the put-in back on the halfway line, which your opponents will almost certainly win. Ask yourself, are the forwards really watching the ball? Remember it's safer to palm the ball only as a variation, if you can get two hands on it catch it and secure possession. Try to persuade your forwards to chase the ball in-field from the touch-line across the sight lines of the receivers – this will improve their chances of winning possession. Remember even the best kick-offs give you only a

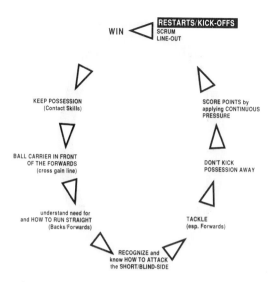

WIN

RESTARTS/KICK-OFFS
SCRUM
LINE-OUT

KEEP POSSESSION
(Contact Skills)

SCORE POINTS by
applying CONTINUOUS
PRESSURE

BALL CARRIER IN FRONT
OF THE FORWARDS
(cross gain line)

DON'T KICK
POSSESSION AWAY

understand need for
and HOW TO RUN STRAIGHT
(Backs/Forwards)

TACKLE
(esp. Forwards)

RECOGNIZE and
know HOW TO ATTACK
the SHORT/BLIND-SIDE

Fig. 3.2

fifty-fifty chance of regaining possession so it's vital that the kicker and the chasing forwards are in tune with each other. You should ask yourself, where can my forwards reasonably be expected to arrive? In other words, how far can they cover in one or two seconds? The kicker should be able to keep the ball in the air for the exact length of time that it will take the forwards to cover the ground to the point where the ball is going to alight. The forwards must follow-up as a unit and in waves and attempt to drive the opponents back off the ball. If you neglect to practise your kick-offs you could be giving away up to a fifth of your set-piece possession and it's a luxury that very few sides can afford.

LINE-OUTS

The line-out is a crucial source of set-ball possession. Often the team that dominates the line-out will be the team that controls the game. Initially, good line-out ball depends on the accuracy of the thrower and the skill of the jumper.

What the three-quarters are looking for is either quick ball . . . or ball delivered while the opposition forwards are in retreat. But it is not just the line-out jumpers that win the

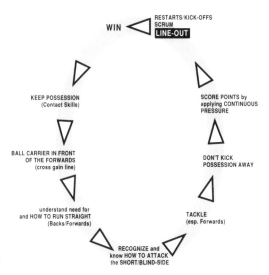

Fig. 3.3

ball, it is the responsibility of every forward; the ball doesn't always go where planned so the reaction time of the whole line-out is crucial. As a general rule never allow your line-out to become predictable, vary the numbers, change the formation particularly if you are being dominated. It always pays to use variations because it frustrates the opposition back row and half backs and keeps them guessing as to what's coming next. Clearly with only three forwards in the Mini Rugby game and five in the Midi Rugby game there are fewer opponents to hinder clean possession of the ball . . . but the above principles apply.

SCRUMS

At all levels all you seek in the scrum is a stable platform and a quick feed of the ball so that the opposition can be attacked whilst they are off balance. Clearly even young players must be prepared for the physical contact in the scrum and they should all be able to handle their own body weight. This means that the good teacher/coach will ensure that they have plenty of simple exercises like press-ups, sit-ups, hand and arm wrestling as part of their necessary preparation. For a scrum to work well it needs good co-ordination between the scrum half

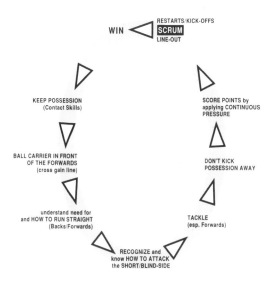

Fig. 3.4

and the hooker. As young players move from the Mini to the Midi Rugby game there is a need to look at variations involving the scrum half, the forwards and the three-quarters. Even at this level, it is important not to become too predictable without in any way losing the major purpose of the scrum, namely to win possession and to win it quickly and cleanly so that the game can be continued.

RETAINING POSSESSION OF THE BALL

Having worked hard to win set ball it is essential that possession is retained. Here the golden rule is one player looks after the ball while the other players look after the ball carrier. Retaining possession calls for a number of contact skills. These are well worth learning because if you have possession of the ball there is no way your opponents can score.

The first and major requirement for retaining possession of the ball is to have good handling skills. Everyone expects the three-quarters to have good hands but winning sides have forwards who are equally adept. Look at your forwards and ask yourself, how many are really comfortable with the ball in their hands? Without good handling from the forwards you will never

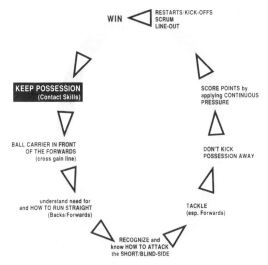

Fig. 3.5

develop continuity in your play: you will always end up with a stop-start-stop type of game which is frustrating to play and boring to watch.

When you make physical contact you need some degree of upper-body strength and technique to hang on to the ball. You certainly don't want the opposition to knock you down and take possession. Therefore you need the strength to stay on your feet and hold off the attack until your support players arrive. Even at Mini level staying on your feet and driving forward requires a certain degree of power in the thighs and seat.

Again there are plenty of hopping, skipping and tug-of-war type activities which can be used for young people with safety. Finally, in retaining possession of the ball it will become apparent to the observant teacher or coach that the young player who most successfully retains possession of the ball normally does so not with an upright body position but with a low aerodynamic driving body position.

Some do this quite naturally, almost as a means of survival, but the majority have to be taught. Whilst most young players retain possession simply and effectively by good handling skills, for the really ambitious they will have to consider weight-training programmes in their late teens, if they are going to optimize their innate skills in the fifteen-a-side game.

GETTING THE BALL CARRIER IN FRONT
OF THE FORWARDS

Having won set ball and retained possession the next priority is to create scoring chances. That is, you need to find ways and means of disrupting the opponent's defence and exploiting the gaps. The key to success lies in getting a ball carrier in front of your forwards, in other words, somebody has to cross the gain line. Good communication between the forwards and backs is essential. If the forwards don't have a feeling for the direction in which the half backs are likely to take the ball either they will be slow to follow up in support or they won't be there at all. This sort of communication has to be developed in your practice sessions, it doesn't just happen.

As your team become more successful in getting a ball carrier in front of the forwards you will notice that the defence becomes disorganized. The next decision is crucial. Do you play close, attack the middle or spin the ball wide? Players at Mini and Midi level who are reading the game correctly will make this sort of decision in a split second. Teams on song tend to have a rhythm which goes pass, pass, penetrate or regroup, pass, pass, penetrate to score. In your preparation you will also have to accept there will be times when the opposition have the ball.

Fig. 3.6

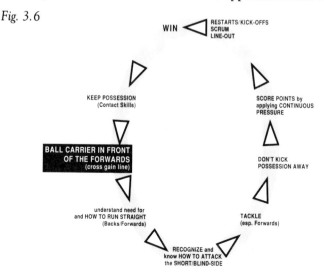

However, it is still possible to apply the principle of getting the ball carrier in front of the forwards even if the opposition have the ball by:

(1)   Catching an opponent in possession of the ball in front of your forwards and then driving him backwards so that he now becomes the ball carrier in front of your forwards.

(2)   The missed touch kick presents the opportunity of regaining possession and for the well-organized team the chance of launching a counter-attack.

In the successful counter attack you will aim to get a ball carrier in front of your forwards so that opponents are drawn to the ball and, at the same time, find themselves back-pedalling towards their own goal line. Remember the principle of the counter attack applies anywhere on the field of play provided you have players who recognize the opportunity when it arises. Now this is a phase of the game which I would earnestly recommend that teachers and coaches do encourage with young players. Teams with their wits about them will recognize when the opposition are vulnerable to a switch of play and it is a marvellous way of encouraging running and handling skills, of quick-witted support play and the ability to make the best use of space. A team of young players who can launch a counter attack really has been well coached and clearly indicates the coach's knowledge and positive attitude of mind at work.

ATTACKING THE SHORT- OR BLIND-SIDE

At Mini and Midi Rugby level, as in the full fifteen-a-side game, there are short- or blind-sides (illustrated in Fig. 3.8) especially from scrum ball and from ruck or maul situations. Here the three-quarters must be alert to the possibility of a short- or blind-side attack and know how to execute it.

Once again, if you see young players being able to recognize and successfully execute attacks down this side of the field it's a clear indication that the person in charge has above average

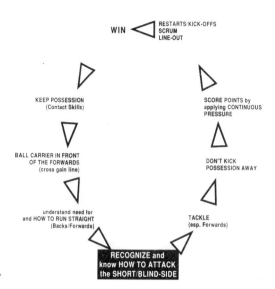

Fig. 3.7

knowledge of the game. At the right moment the advantages of attacking the blind-side are many; it's the least defended side of the field, fewer passes are required and, finally, the principal support players, the forwards, do not have far to run in support of the ball carrier. Remember, attacking the short-side requires planning and its effectiveness is directly related to the speed of its execution, surprise is everything.

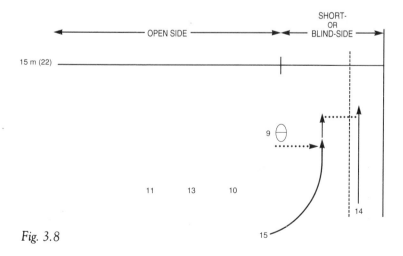

Fig. 3.8

STRAIGHT RUNNING

One of the means of getting a ball carrier in front of the forwards is by running straight. The ability to run straight achieves
many objectives; you take out opponents, create space on either
side of the ball carrier and consequently increase your attacking
options. The secret of straight running is to get on to your
intended running line before you receive the ball. Remember,
individual defenders will be coming up on your inside shoulder
trying to force you out towards the touch-line. Therefore if you
are on a straight running line before you receive the ball you
will have a much better chance of forcing one or more of the
opposition to commit themselves to tackling you, thus creating
space for your support players to exploit. Naturally, everyone
associates straight running with the three-quarters but forwards
can also run straight to devastating effect. The key for the
forwards is to develop that basic instinct to come in-field from
the touch-line so as to open up the options of attacking the
short-side as well as the open-side. You would therefore tend
to say to a forward who had the ball in his hands, 'Make for
the near goal post.'

A simple piece of advice for your young players in particular
is to tell them that they should imagine that there is an electric

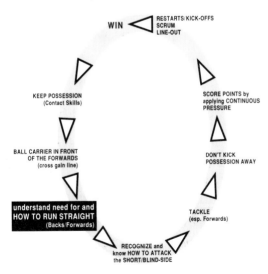

Fig. 3.9

fence running down each side of the pitch – or that the touchline is the sixteenth player who should be avoided at all costs. Perhaps one of these pieces of information will persuade them to make for their opponent's near goal post! Remember always tell the ball carrier to get ahead of his forwards. This simple action will improve the ability of supporting players to do their job.

KICKING LOSES POSSESSION

It is only at the end of the Mini Rugby phase in England that the Under Elevens are introduced to kicking. Some would argue that this is too early, others would argue it's too late. Whatever the answer, there is no doubt that kicking is often used by players when they feel they are running out of space, almost as an act of desperation. By the very act of kicking a ball you lose possession of it. The teacher/coach and player have to therefore ask themselves the following questions:

(1)   Why am I kicking the ball?

(2)   Where am I kicking it?

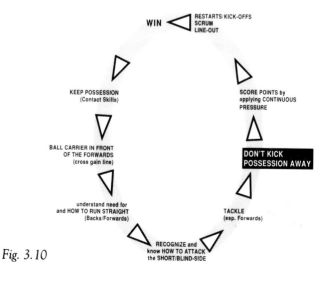

Fig. 3.10

(3)   What type of kick am I going to use?

(4)   Who is chasing that kick so that the kicker's team have every reasonable chance of regaining possession?

The one thing you can rest assured of is that a misplaced kick is never going to win any friends amongst the forwards. In any team it is normally the scrum half, fly half, inside centre, occasionally the wings and frequently the full back who kick the ball – they should certainly have answers to the above questions.

Unless the kicker practises with the rest of the team so that everyone is aware of when the kick is about to take place and where it is going to then there is no conceivable way in which the kick will be properly supported. As a teacher or coach if you are going to introduce kicking to young players (5, 6, 7, 8, 9 years) you would be advised, in the first instance, to let them kick for distance or height in order to develop a 'full' range of movement – do not worry about accuracy. However, thereafter ensure they have a target, use cones to mark out the landing area and be realistic, make the practice as near to the game as you possibly can.

THE REFEREE

In any understanding of the game it is only the foolish teacher/coach or player who does not take into his planning the major impact and the importance of the referee. Not only is he the sole judge of fact and law during the game, but like the players he is giving of his time on a voluntary basis as part of his recreation. Always be polite, never back-chat the referee and do exactly as he says. If he doesn't like what you are doing – change tactics. Play to the laws that he is refereeing whether you agree or not. He is in total charge.

SUMMARY OR CHECKLIST

(1)   A WINNING TEAM wins its own scrums, line-outs and kick-offs.

(2)   A WINNING TEAM keeps possession of the ball.

(3)   A WINNING TEAM gets a ball carrier across the game line.

(4)   A WINNING TEAM has players who know how to run straight.

(5)   A WINNING TEAM knows how to attack the short- or blind-side.

(6)   A WINNING TEAM tackles, particularly among the forwards.

(7)   A WINNING TEAM doesn't kick possession away but it does kick its goals.

(8)   A WINNING TEAM doesn't give its opponents time or space, they are always under pressure.

(9)   If you want to be a part of a WINNING TEAM you should take nothing for granted. Winning is a matter of planning, preparation and a very positive attitude of mind.

(10)   WINNERS set high standards not only for themselves but for the whole team – strive for the elimination of mistakes and strive for EXCELLENCE.

4

BEING IN CONTROL

Now that you have some feel for the ethos or spirit of the game where cheating is not acceptable, and are beginning to grasp the crucial importance of having a wide and deep understanding of the game, which will govern every practice session that you run and systematically help you to develop a winning team, it's time to look at 'teaching methods'. In other words how you exercise CONTROL. Without this ability, whatever knowledge you have will never find expression.

The qualified teacher has normally spent a minimum of four years finding out the theory of how youngsters learn and what they are capable of learning, depending on their age. Throughout their career any self-respecting teacher will tell you that they always learn something new even after twenty years in the job. Let me give you a simple example. If you face a group of seven or eight year olds, all of whom are holding a rugby ball, and you say in all innocence (or naïvety) to the group, 'Right, give me a ball,' you will probably be hit with at least six balls thrown at the same time. You need to be very specific. 'Simon, and only Simon, bring me your ball.' The better your ability to teach or control a group the more chance the group have of understanding what you want of them.

Perhaps in an ideal situation you would weigh every boy so that at least in the learning stages only those of equal weight worked together. Because this is neither practicable nor usually necessary, the simple rule of thumb that teachers have applied for many years is to divide the class or group according to their height which, in teaching as opposed to match circumstances, generally ensures that the very light boy is not competing against a very heavy boy. However, the following photograph, from a quite magnificent RFU publication called *Even Better Rugby*, does illustrate different body types and, therefore, the physical problem when dealing with eleven- and twelve-year-old boys.

As I have indicated, match circumstances are quite different from the teaching situation. If you have a boy who dwarfs all others and he has the strength and co-ordination to equal his size, then, whilst it is extremely tempting to use him to annihilate the opposition, common sense must prevail. This one boy could so demoralize the opposition that they don't want to play rugby again – this I have seen happen! Please use him sparingly, ideally with those of his own size but, where this is not possible, at least put him on the wing so that the rest have to work the ball to him, or condition him so that he is only allowed to score *one* try in *each half*!

Remember . . .

Skill and not physique should dominate this stage of the learning process.

Another important teaching aid is to use grids and channels. These are simple yet effective areas of work which allow you maximum control of what may be quite a large group.

There is nothing magical about grids and channels *per se*, and as there are many ways to skin a cat or routes up a mountain, then I am sure there must be plenty of ways of teaching rugby successfully. Nevertheless, grids/channels do have a number of

Illus. 1: These boys are all eleven years of age!

marked advantages in that the group are working in small, well-defined areas, all within the vision of the teacher, and they do offer as good an opportunity as I can think of to allow the teacher to teach and not merely occupy the youngsters' time.

Frequently practices are useless unless they are carried out within the pressure of a clearly defined area. Do not forget space, or lack of it, equals time, equals pressure. If you don't believe me ask anyone who has played international rugby and they will tell you one of two things: either that mistakes which they got away with at club level were ruthlessly punished, or the speed of the game at international level was such that they had little time or space in which to think. In other words, they were under much greater pressure than they were used to at club level. Grids and channels, depending on their size, create either more or less pressure on the players. In the early stages of using grids you will not only have to show physically each group which grid they are working in but, no doubt, you will also have to keep reminding them of the need to stick within the boundaries of their own grid.

In operating grids, the best advice I can pass on to Mini/Midi Rugby coaches is the advice I was given at college. Imagine that you are in a gymnasium and 'keep your back to the wall'. Never give your instructions from the middle of the grid system because you will be forever turning round to see everyone or else only

Fig. 4.1

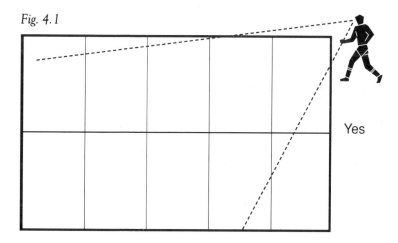

Yes

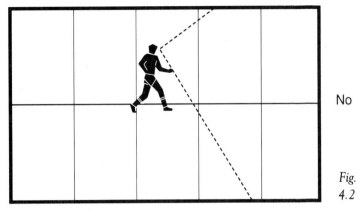

No

Fig.
4.2

half the class will see your face at any one time and that spells trouble as far as your ability to control the group is concerned.

Without control there cannot be effective teaching and this is one of the prime functions of the Mini/Midi Rugby coach. In a rugby context, it is worth reminding you that 'teaching' is the imparting of new techniques, and 'coaching' is the polishing process. For example, a boy may have been taught the basic pass and know the key factors of the technique. However, when he comes to pass the ball against opposition the accuracy of his pass leaves much to be desired. Coaching now takes over and the observant helper will have spotted, for example, that the player does not look where he is passing.

Having analysed what was wrong, you must now prescribe a remedy – incidentally, this is what we call 'diagnosis'. By asking the player to turn his head and look where he is passing, he will at least give the ball carrier an opportunity of seeing the target he is aiming at and so have a better chance of passing the ball 'out in front' of the receiver's chest. Information like this is so easy to deliver to the boy who requires it without upsetting the rhythm of the whole group. All you have to do is to go into any particular grid, ask that particular group to stop whilst the other grids continue to work, and give your instructions.

Every teacher or coach worth their salt will spend a considerable time preparing their material. Proper planning and preparation will be rewarded by the way youngsters respond. Teaching and coaching are most worthwhile activities.

PREPARATION

Do . . .

(1)   Consider the age, ability and experience of the players.

This advice came home to me most forcibly during the early part of my career when I took a group of seven-year-olds, including one of my own sons, every Sunday morning from September to December. First of all, I was not short of ideas on small-side games and practices, but none of them worked for the simple reason that few could catch the ball and only two boys could run and pass the ball to each other without dropping it! All of my previous practical experience had been with boys of secondary school age or senior players, and this reminded me most strongly that I needed to take into account the AGE, ABILITY and EXPERIENCE of the players before proceeding any further. For those who have found themselves in a similar situation, i.e., working with six and seven year olds, they will have discovered that boys of this age are absolute chatterboxes and obsessed with being paired or grouped with their best friend(s). As a result, they do not listen to instructions. I found that it was essential to run them around sufficiently in order that they were puffing and panting (this was in fact part of their warm-up!). Only then did they stop talking and begin to listen. What I found worked particularly well with this age group was ball carrying relays, but instead of dividing the group into two, which means that most are standing and shouting encouragement to fellow team members, I divided them into as many groups of three or four to a team as was possible.

Do . . .

(2)   Decide upon realistic targets or aims to be achieved in the time available.

Do not assume that in any one session you are going to teach all that there is to know about, for example, hooking, with and against the put-in. Setting yourself realistic targets is so important because if you attempt too much then all you will probably achieve is confusion in the minds of the players. Only move on to the next stage or progression when the first one has been understood.

Do . . .

(3)   Produce an outline for the whole season/course, bearing in mind the facilities and equipment required.

In academic subjects like chemistry, mathematics or geography, the head of department would almost certainly have drawn up a syllabus of work to be covered in each term, each year, indeed to cover the whole period of a child's time in that particular school. Incorporated into this syllabus would be the number of books, charts, films, etc., required in order to ensure the smooth running of the syllabus.

At the end of each year a review of the syllabus would take place to see how it had operated, whether changes needed to be made to improve the presentation of the existing material, or whether new developments had taken place which rendered some of the existing material obsolete. Assistant teachers would have access to this syllabus and be invited to make a contribution to its construction.

Perhaps it is pie in the sky to expect this degree of preparation to take place with Mini/Midi Rugby, but happily there are some clubs now moving in this direction. Again, if people are going to give hours of their recreation time to help promote rugby for young players then it makes sense to plan the programme thoroughly so as to maximize the time and ability of both helpers and players. This type of planning will also ensure that when a helper leaves the area the whole scheme continues to run smoothly and does not come to an abrupt end as has happened in some clubs. Don't live from hand to mouth!

Do . . .

(4)   Prepare each session carefully – select the material to be covered and consider how it will be presented.

AIM: to give an enjoyable, active introduction to Rugby Football

Lesson Plan	Task	Teaching points & Technique	Organization
Warm-up			
1. Free activity			
2. Relay			
Contact			
Individual skill			
Unit skill (Not applicable in first lesson)			
Team skill e.g. short game of Touch or End ball			

Fig. 4.3

Notes on the development of the Lesson:
As soon as the lesson is finished, it will help future planning if some brief notes are made. Some skills may be particularly bad or some ideas not developed which must be used in subsequent lessons.

Assuming there is a master plan, a syllabus, call it what you will, it should be possible for helpers to know what work they should have covered up to that moment in time.

This makes the task of preparing the next session so much easier. The recommended framework for each session is shown in Fig. 4.3.

Having decided the material that you would like to cover in the next session, decide how it best will be presented. For example, are demonstrations necessary? (And, remember, unless you personally can give a good demonstration, find someone else.) Do I need to work in small groups? Would a video save hours of explanation?

These and many other points must be considered before the session.

Do . . .

(5)   Memorize the material and the key factors to be empha-
        sized – prepare reminder notes for your clipboard.

Like so many people, I have found over the years that 'mental rehearsal' and a few notes covering the key points that I wish to make have been invaluable. Memorizing the material with just the odd glance at your notes is arguably the best way of convincing your audience that you've prepared the session. What is not acceptable, in my opinion, is to be seen rushing up and down the pitch carrying a clipboard and to be constantly referring to it. Leave the clipboard at the side of the pitch and take the odd glance if you really feel it necessary. Really, you should be responding to the players and not your clipboard!

Let me make one or two comments about *key factors*. In a rugby context look upon them as being *the absolutely essential information given in the fewest words possible in order to have the maximum effect.*

If we are teaching a group of youngsters the basic pass we would say, 'Put the ball out in front of the receiver's chest.' Now, if this information is accompanied by a demonstration then the key factors can be abbreviated even further, thus: take the ball early, swing your arms, ball out in front of the receiver. This same approach can be adopted for all basic and positional techniques/skills of the game, and of course, for the unit skills.

Do . . .

(6)   Ensure that you have enough equipment for everyone
        and that it is readily available.

I suppose this advice is so obvious that it should not need
mentioning, but not having enough rugby balls for the numbers
involved or the chosen activity is so common an oversight that
it is worthy of a further reminder.

Again, a scrummage machine is such an invaluable aid in
the early stages of learning the various positional responsibilities of scrummaging, or introducing back-row moves from a
stable platform, that no club/school should be without one.
You don't necessarily have to go to the expense of buying a
whole machine; the head of a machine fixed to the wall and
floor will suffice.

Plastic cones, which we've used at our Twickenham coaching
demonstrations before all major matches, are another invaluable
and relatively cheap item of equipment. With them you can
quickly mark out grids or channels, or even a whole pitch.

Having recently visited Japan, I returned with a few ideas
which I have not seen in operation in this country and as
with all good ideas they are remarkably simple. They concern
playing equipment. In Japan, such is the pressure on pitches
that a few hundred children have to use the same pitch on a
rota basis and, as a result, there is not a blade of grass to be
seen anywhere. Obviously, the climate and topography of the
country play a big part in this state of affairs but, believe me,
when the wind blows the grounds resemble the Kalahari Desert
and when it rains, paddy fields.

Consequently, the Japanese Rugby Union has a rule that all
youngsters must wear scrum caps. Now, the caps are thicker
than ours and come in the basic colours, that is, red, blue,
green, etc. Not only do these caps provide protection against
the hard grounds (much more frequent than soft pitches) but,
because of their colours, matches are played, for example,
between red scrum caps and blue scrum caps; by this means
the identification of the teams is very simple.

Scrum caps in Japan are a lot cheaper than shirts. I visited a session one Sunday morning at the Kyoto Rugby School and the organization, like the colours, was dazzling.

Each boy who joined the school purchased a shirt and on the back of his shirt he stitched his club number, for example 47. On the front of his shirt he stitched the club badge and, in the space provided, he wrote his own name. This idea is so simple and yet helps enormously the problem of putting a name to a face which can be very difficult, if, as some clubs in England have found, they have three hundred boys turning up for the Mini Rugby sessions.

From a distance, therefore, a coach could spot a number on a boy's back, memorize it and then, at his leisure, find out the boy's name so as to note whether, for example, he was a talented player or someone who needed extra help.

Having done your preparation thoroughly you can easily slip up by not really understanding how to effectively present your material. Here are a few hints.

PRESENTATION

Do . . .

(1)   Show confidence in your ability and enthusiasm for the game.

It's a fairly safe bet that whatever standard you aspired to as a player, you will at least have more knowledge than the fledgling Mini/Midi Rugby players. Enthusiasm can be infectious and it can certainly take you a long way. At the same time, enthusiasm must be tempered with knowledge and there is no doubt in my mind that many who help with Mini/Midi Rugby would benefit enormously from taking an RFU Start Rugby course open to both men and women.

Do . . .

(2)   Ensure that you have good control of the group – insist on close attention when you are speaking.

Now, pay attention for this really is important. Never

speak unless your audience is watching you and they are silent. Make sure that you haven't positioned the group so that the sun is shining in their eyes, or that a bevy of girls in frilly knickers (or whatever the equivalent is in a girl's world) are immediately behind you as the group, quite naturally, will watch the girls instead of you! As with work in grids, do not stand so that you are ringed by the group – make certain they are in a semicircle or in a line.

If you are dealing with a large group and you are either demonstrating yourself or have arranged someone else to demonstrate, then you would probably be advised to ask the group to squat down. On the other hand, if you are showing them the position of the head in a side tackle with both the tackler and the tackled player on their knees, then they will normally see better if they are standing up.

When demonstrating a side-step or swerve, don't let the players watch from the side but from either in front, or better still, behind. Why? The running lines and the position of the feet are so much more obvious from this viewpoint, and therefore, more easily copied.

Really be quite specific in your instructions. If you say, 'Run round the cones or round the goal posts,' do not be surprised if they do an Indian war dance round a particular object. Perhaps what you really meant to say was, 'Run round the outside of . . . all of the cones . . . the cones in your grid . . . run in a clockwise direction round the outside of the cones.' I am sorry if I am teaching my grandmother how to suck eggs, but it is so important to have control of the group – *before* you begin.

Do . . .

(3) Ensure your voice is clear, stimulating and varied in volume, pace, pitch and emphasis.

There is an actor or actress in every good teacher or coach and the voice is a remarkably important 'instrument' by which communications are established and the resultant actions executed. Famous words like:

Now is the winter of our discontent
Made glorious summer by this sun of York

from Shakespeare's *Richard III*, can be totally drab and flat
until mouthed by a Laurence Olivier or Kenneth Branagh.
Suddenly, they have a new meaning and vibrance. Obviously,
we can't all be Laurence Olivier or Kenneth Branagh, but we
can use and develop the talents we were born with. Remember
what I said in Chapter Two – education is about 'lighting fires
and not filling jugs'. Your choice can kindle that fire.

It is no use delivering all your instructions in a dead-pan
voice or in a strident one. Particular actions that you expect
of the players will demand speed, strength, power, subtlety,
etc. Your voice should reflect these qualities.

Do . . .

(4)   Use demonstrations and visual aids to assist under-
       standing.

One good demonstration can save hours of explanation.
Visual aids, like video tape, 35 mm slides, overhead pro-
jector acetates, blackboard and chalk used sensibly can also
save invaluable time. You can purchase a rugby video that
shows youngsters how international players perform a particular
skill.

If someone in your club has a video camera you can
film a practice session or a match, and, after studying it
carefully yourself beforehand, you can then show it to the
players. You will have to let them see it at least once
through with few comments from yourself, because when
players have never seen themselves before on the screen they
are so fascinated and excited that they don't really 'see' what
they are doing right or wrong. When the novelty has worn off
then you can begin to use the video as intended, namely, to
compliment them on their good points and to train their inner
eye to be much more observant. Even international players will
not believe you if you tell them that they never used their left
foot in the match, they always side-stepped to the right, they
missed seeing two overlaps, etc. Show them on the screen and

it's a different story.

Do not be too gimmicky with your visual aids – be realistic and ask yourself, 'Am I helping the player(s) to see more clearly what it is that I want them to do?'

Do . . .

(5)   Keep instructions brief and emphasize only the key factors you want players to concentrate on.

Much of this I have already touched upon. Using the illustration of the basic pass again and comparing how it is taught nowadays with, say, twenty to twenty-five years ago: remember – take the ball early, swing your arms and ball out in front of the receiver? When I was at school, and this is really giving the game away, I was told that when passing to my left I had to make sure that when my right foot hit the ground I took my arms and the ball across the right side of my body. In the next stage, as my left foot came through it had to be planted in front of but across my right leg and, at the same time, the ball was swung across my body from right to left. This complete action was practised in waltz time down the length of the field. Now you know why today you are asked to keep the instructions brief and emphasize only the key factors!

Do not . . .

(1)   Neglect some players to concentrate on others – delegate the captain or pack leader to control activities of players you cannot supervise.

Just remember, the players will soon spot who are your favourites even if you are unaware yourself that you have been concentrating on a few at the expense of the majority. Whilst it is difficult to delegate matters of a technical nature to Mini/Midi Rugby players because they simply do not have the knowledge or experience of the game, it is still possible to encourage qualities of leadership through inviting those with obvious initiative to help supervise the others: ensuring that the equipment is on the field and locked up again, that a roll call has taken place – these and other small but necessary chores can be undertaken by the players thus giving you more time to concentrate on your real task, that is, to teach. Incidentally, if you can train a player(s) to captain a side or lead a pack in a sensible and thoughtful manner you will be doing the side and the game a big favour. Most young captains or pack leaders mouth words without the faintest idea of what they are saying, let alone whether they are saying them at the right time or to the right player.

Do not . . .

(2)   Talk too much.

(3)   Nag – encouragement brings the best response.

Remember . . .

(1)   Enjoyment and maximum participation are vital.

If you remember the simple maxim that 'you learn through purposeful activity', you won't go far wrong. Also, do not necessarily equate enjoyment with a smile on the face. Some players are never happier than when you are putting them through hell. In fact, in my experience, no matter what the age, no player will thank you if he is underworked. I've had them barely able to crawl off the field and, much to my surprise, they have said how much they enjoyed the session . . . mind you, that's generally after a bath and a pint (orange naturally)!

Remember . . .

(2)   Variety of material and presentation are essential.

Read, watch international matches, ask experienced players the wrinkles of their position, attend coaching courses – there is no easy way of building up your knowledge and it cannot be acquired overnight.

On the other hand, there are some who are veritable mines of information but they do not know how to present their material. Mini/Midi Rugby coaches who are often former players, quite often fall into this category. They have had no formal training in teaching skills and they become frustrated or simply do not do themselves justice. Apart from attending courses, try and get along to watch a good club coach in action.

Remember . . .

(3)   Practice must be related to the game.

After you have taught a particular technique you will naturally develop it so that it becomes a skill which the player can demonstrate in a game. Or will you? Sadly, few coaches set up practices which really do relate to what the player will have to contend with in the game. They get through the technique stage quite well, for example, they may have taught successfully a side-step from right to left against passive opposition, a body or a post. Now comes the difficult bit because there is nowhere in a game that a player is called upon to side-step a stationary body, let alone a post.

Let us think of a match situation.

Scrum on the halfway line 15 metres from their right touch-line – team X, playing down the pitch, are putting the ball in, which naturally will be on their left side of the scrum. The easy way for the scrum half to pass is to his right, which he does. The fly half takes it flat and moving right about 7 metres from the scrum. His opposite number has come across in anticipation but too slowly, so our outside half easily beats him on the outside. In the meanwhile our defending team's full back is covering across and is intent on pushing the outside half of team X towards the touch-line. Unfortunately for the full back the fly half had been taught to side-step from right to left and this is what he proceeds to do.

Now, your task as the Mini/Midi Rugby coach is to set up this match situation with every player in their correct position and only moving at the correct time. So often, the inexperienced coach allows players, and particularly defending players, to take up false positions because they are anticipating where the action is going to be. Do not allow yourself to be sucked into this trap otherwise your practice will not be related to the game and its value will be nil.

Remember . . .

(4)   Motivation will lift performance – but it can be overdone.

This section alone is worthy of a book. All I would say is the obvious. All players are different in their physical, mental and psychological make-up and each will react differently to the same stimulus. The best motivation that anyone involved in Mini/Midi Rugby can foster is the one whereby an individual is so inspired that they actually want to learn more about the game and practise to improve their game in their own time.

As this reminder implies, some coaches do seem to motivate players to an absurd degree. Hating the opposition is not what the game wants or needs. In the end, the best motivation is self-orientated because in this way individuals will commit themselves as I've suggested above.

Remember . . .

(5)   Encourage players to think and mentally rehearse their skills, this will bring improvements in performance.

This is another facet of self-motivation which is obviously easier to carry out with older players because it is very difficult to rehearse skills until the players have been taught enough of them and have a reasonably wide vocabulary. Nevertheless, eleven- and twelve-year-olds who have had three seasons' experience of rugby should be encouraged to think for themselves, for example, of how to cope if the scrum is wheeled. Obviously players should physically practise this as well but mental rehearsal for the player is just as important as it is for the coach.

Remember . . .

(6)   Success in the game will be determined by the player making the right decisions. Understanding the game means a player will be aware of all the options available to him.

I would add a rider to this which says, 'The worst decision you can make is to make no decision at all.' Mini/Midi Rugby is the breeding ground where decision-making is incubated and, hopefully, hatched. Nowhere is the quality of the coaching more cruelly exposed than in this one area. Wooden-headed players are invariably a product of the unthinking teacher or coach.

In simple terms, there are three processes in the making of effective decisions.

First of all the player, and let us assume it is the fly half, has to read the display in front of him. For example, if there is a scrum on the centre of his own 15-metre line (equivalent to the 22-metre line in the fifteen-a-side game) and his team are putting the ball in, the player has to make a note of where opposition players are standing, whether his opposite number is quick and decisive in the tackle, the weather conditions, particularly the wind, and remember whether or not his own scrum half can pass only one way or both and the length of his pass. Secondly, having made a mental note of these points, the player must now come to a decision. Let us say, for argument's sake, that he has decided that he will take the ball going right and kick it directly into touch from inside the 15-metre area and so gain ground for his forwards – now, whether this was the correct decision or not, given the disposition of the opposition, we will not concern ourselves at this stage but assume for this example that it was.

The third and final stage is now upon him. The player has interpreted the display and made a decision. Now the brain must tell the relevant parts of the anatomy to kick the ball accurately up field so that it crosses the right-hand touch-line as far up the field as possible. Supposing, however, the ball is sliced badly so that it either lands down the opposition full back's throat or the ball actually goes behind. Obviously, this will not be looked upon very favourably by team-mates, but this is not the point I am really stressing.

In making decisions or reading the game, a mistake can be made in any one of these three stages. The outside half could have put a wrong interpretation on the display. Even if absolutely correct in what was seen, the player may have chosen the wrong option. Perhaps in the example above the fly half should have run with the ball rather than have kicked it.

Finally, the player can read the display correctly, come to the right decision and then, as we have seen because of technical deficiencies, is unable to execute a simple skill like kicking the ball out of the hand with the right foot whilst on the move.

From all of this you can see that the coach not only has to know the game in great detail, but also how decisions are arrived at.

I deliberately choose the fly half position in my example because I believe that in a practice situation not only should the coach stand close to and behind the fly half, but should give as many of the Mini/Midi Rugby players as possible an opportunity to play in this most important decision-making position.

NOTES FOR GUIDANCE OF CANDIDATES ON TEACHING METHOD

Note: This is the basic checklist that candidates taking the RFU Start Pack or Preliminary Award would be reminded of.

PREPARATION

Do . . .

(1)   Consider the age, ability and experience of the players.

(2)   Decide upon realistic targets or aims to be achieved in the time available.

(3)   Produce an outline for the whole season/course, bearing in mind the facilities and equipment required.

(4)   Prepare each session carefully – select the material to be covered and consider how it will be presented.

(5)   Memorize the material and the key factors to be emphasized – prepare reminder notes for your clipboard.

(6)   Ensure that you have enough equipment for everyone and that it is readily available.

PRESENTATION

Do . . .

(1)   Show confidence in your ability and enthusiasm for the game.

(2)   Ensure that you have good control of the group – insist on close attention when you are speaking.

(3)   Ensure your voice is clear, stimulating and varied in volume, pace, pitch and emphasis.

(4)   Use demonstrations and visual aids to assist understanding.

(5)   Keep instructions brief and emphasize only the key factors you want players to concentrate upon.

Do not . . .

(1)   Neglect some players to concentrate on others – delegate the captain or pack leader to control activities of players you cannot supervise.

(2)   Talk too much.

(3)   Nag – encouragement brings the best response.

Remember . . .

(1)   Enjoyment and maximum participation are vital.

(2)   Variety of material and presentation are essential.

(3)   Practice must be related to the game.

(4)   Motivation will lift performance – but it can be overdone.

(5)   Encourage players to think and mentally rehearse their skills, this will bring improvements in performance.

(6)   Success in the game will be determined by the player making the right decisions. Understanding the game means a player will be aware of all the options available.

ALL SKILLS TO ALL PLAYERS

5

WARM UP – COOL DOWN

There is an unfortunate tendency to assume that because a coach is dealing with young children and the latter tend to fall and bounce back up like an indiarubber ball, there is no need to inflict a warm-up upon them. Not so. All muscles require to be warm and stretched if they are to perform optimally. Take a look at your dog or cat when they have woken up from a sleep. What do they do? Well, unless they are unusual, they will stretch the long muscles of their back and generally perform animal calisthenics before moving off. The human body requires the same treatment. Persuading youngsters to form good habits at a tender age will stand them in excellent stead long after their rugby careers are merely glazed memories.

It's best to begin with some gentle running to promote and raise body temperatures followed by stretching exercises. These should be performed before and after each session. Yes, a cool-down is as important as a warm-up! A cool-down helps remove the waste products of exercise and consequently reduces the amount of stiffness which frequently occurs after a hard exercise session. Incidentally, stretching should be controlled, and not a series of bouncing or explosive movements. Finally, either begin at the ankles and work upwards or at the head and neck and work downwards. In this way you will tend not to forget any of the large muscle groups.

PHYSICAL CONDITIONING

The following are Body Conditioning Exercises to prepare young players (pre-puberty) for fitness training sessions and the rigours of Mini Rugby in order to minimize injury by:

(1)   Preparing tendons and ligaments for the increased muscle bulk of puberty; thereby retaining a healthy state of flexibility.

(2)   Strengthening the major muscle groups which protect internal organs and vulnerable joints.

(3)   Learning how to use muscles in order to improve ACTIONS.

These exercises can be performed at home, or in changing rooms, club houses etc., prior to taking the pitch and are recommended to be carried out three times per week. If fathers join in they can check that the exercises are correctly performed, motivate by example, and as a by-product do themselves a great deal of good as the exercises are ideal for post thirty-five years, when old injuries causing symptoms such as lower back ache begin to affect mobility.

LIMBERING

This means loosening prior to warming-up exercises.

(Training shoes or bare feet – Standing)

(1)   Shake out legs in downwards relaxed manner. Loose long arms. Right then left, etc.

(2)   Plant feet (1 foot apart)
(a)   wobble thighs like blancmanges, then;
(b)   wobble buttocks.

(3)   Plant feet. Circle shoulders backwards one at a time, and then both together smoothly.

(4)   Limbering step on the spot; toes in contact with the floor, HEELS up and down alternately touching the floor on each down stroke to stimulate the achilles tendon.

(5)   Knees bent, feet parallel 10 inches apart. Arms held out in front at chest level. ROCK from heels to toes and back smoothly and continuously, with weight transferred on OUTSIDE HALF of the feet (Fig. 5.1).

Fig. 5.1

Coach Watch For (Limbering Section)

(1)   Long neck and relaxed shoulders.

(2)   (a)   Front of thighs like jelly;
        (b)   Buttocks like jelly.

(3)   Long neck, relaxed action.

(4)   Heels touch floor every time. Hips to the side on each 'step'.

(5)   Knees stay over feet throughout and *do not* move inwards towards each other.

STRETCHING

(1)   Start with feet apart – toes out-turned. Slowly move knee out over right foot, stretching left leg. Return to centre and move over left foot (Fig. 5.2).

Fig. 5.2

(2)   Drop down over right foot (Fig. 5.3). Point and flex left foot six times. Return slowly to centre and repeat over left foot.

(3)   Adopt position as shown in Fig. 5.4 and slowly bend and straighten knees. Weight on finger tips.

(4)   **Scythe** – adopt position as shown in Fig. 5.5. Knees

Fig. 5.3

Fig. 5.4

bent throughout, arms held straight and parallel with shoulders. Swing round and behind lifting hands to ear level, then down and forward to knee level in front, then round the other side.

Fig. 5.5

(5) **Hamstring stretch** – boy lies on back, one knee bent, foot on floor. Raise other leg straight and hold behind calf muscle. Gently pull own leg towards head. Six gentle pulls and change legs. (See Fig. 5.6).

Fig. 5.6

Coach Watch For (Stretching Section)

(1)   Make sure knees move over foot in perfect line. Keep the exercise smooth and slow. Fig. 5.2.

(2)   Keep head up and foot of bent leg pointing forward. Fig. 5.3.

(3)   Head up. Smooth action for gradual stretching of aductors. Fig. 5.4.
        Eventually palms may be kept on the floor.

(4)   Easy swing. Boy feels power of his thigh and buttocks. Fig. 5.5.

(5)   Do not attempt to pull leg for boy. Let him find his own degree of flexibility. Fig. 5.6.

STRENGTHENING

Learning the correct use of buttocks (glutial muscles), abdominal sheet, thighs and long extensors of the back. These are the 'power' muscles of the body and will be used for pushing, jumping, driving in (ruck/maul) and during the receiving of tackles. Correct use will protect internal organs and the lower back.

(1)   **Abdominal suck** (Fig.5.7) – stand, feet parallel, knees bent and stomach totally relaxed, hands on hips. As you straighten knees, suck in whole of abdominal sheet, i.e., from ribs to pelvis. Hold contraction and relax. Repeat six times, then tense abdomen and make

Fig. 5.7

fists like a boxer about to receive a body blow. Relax
and repeat whole sequence.

(2)   **Buttock contractions** (Fig.5.8) – same as (1) except
the buttocks are contracting and hardening.

Fig. 5.8

(3)   **Pre' sit up** (Fig.5.9) – lie on back, knees bent,
hands above head on the floor. Contract abdominals
as you raise hands slowly towards knees – raise head
with chin on chest so that boy looks at knees. Keep
hands 2 inches above floor outside knees. Then slowly
return and relax shoulders. Repeat six times.

Fig. 5.9

(4)   **Conditioning sit up** (Fig. 5.10) – contract abdominals
        and sit up. Count 4, lie down and place hands flat on
        the floor by side. Contract buttocks and raise. Hold for
        a count of 4 and repeat sequence ten times.

Fig. 5.10

(5)   **Spinal support** – lie on stomach – hands stretched
        out in front. Raise right hand and left leg and head
        at the same time and hold up. Relax and then raise
        the opposite limbs.

This exercise prepares the supporting muscles of the spine.

Coach Watch For (Strengthening Section)

(1) Boy's 'navel' should move in and out about 4 inches. Feel abdomen during boxer stance to check firmness. Fig. 5.7.

(2) Boy keeps knees parallel throughout. Develop a firm strong stance. Fig. 5.8.

(3) Make sure boy keeps chin on chest as he raises head to avoid strain around neck. Fig. 5.9.

(4) Keep elbows straight on 'sit up'. Slide hands up thighs to reach knees. Remember chin on chest as before. Fig. 5.10.

(5) Smooth change, no jerking necessary.

PROTECTION MOVEMENTS

(1) Stand up straight, interlock fingers at chest level. Turn backs of hands towards chest and push out

Fig. 5.11

forwards and hold. Grip strongly in buttocks and raise outstretched and joined hands upwards above head. Take hands behind head twice still gripping hard in buttocks. Release fingers and let arms float down to start again at chest level. (See Fig. 5.11.)

(2)   Face boy and place flat of hands on either side of his head over each ear. Boy nods six times to the right and six times to the left against the slight resistance of your hands. Then place hand on boy's forehead and allow him to nod forward against this resistance.

(3)   Lie on floor on back completely relaxed. Roll head to right and left slowly with mouth slightly open and eyes closed. Keep shoulders very relaxed.

Coach Watch For

(1)   The contracting buttocks will protect the boy's lower back as he pushes his arms behind his head. He will find this useful when scrummaging. Fig. 5.11.

(2)   Offer only a slight resistance. The boy may be standing or sitting.

These body conditioning exercises are designed to minimize injury by:

(1)   Preparing tendons and ligaments for the increased muscle bulk of puberty; thereby retaining a healthy state of flexibility.

(2)   Strengthening the major muscle groups which protect internal organs and vulnerable joints.

(3)   Learning how to use muscles in order to improve ACTIONS.

Don't finish any session abruptly. Cool down. Go for a gentle run and stretch; this will help the body to recover by slowly ridding itself of waste products of exercise like lactic acid.

6

HANDLING

All young players will come to your session hoping to enjoy themselves. To achieve this simple aim they must participate in some form of play. As early as possible, therefore, they must be involved in purposeful activity. You should devote the time available in the following way.

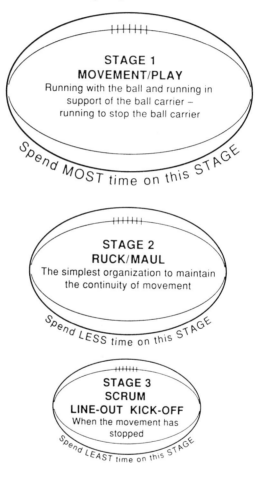

STAGE 1
MOVEMENT/PLAY
Running with the ball and running in
support of the ball carrier –
running to stop the ball carrier

Spend MOST time on this STAGE

STAGE 2
RUCK/MAUL
The simplest organization to maintain
the continuity of movement

Spend LESS time on this STAGE

STAGE 3
SCRUM
LINE-OUT KICK-OFF
When the movement has
stopped

Spend LEAST time on this STAGE

Fig. 6.1

You should have reached that point in your preparation where you have decided in your own mind why you've volunteered to help young players enjoy their recreation, this is crucially important to the young and their progress. You have tried hard to understand how much effort goes into winning, not only the obvious physical efforts on the field but the mental application off it; you've armed yourself with some simple communication skills (being in control) and you are now faced with your first group of eager youngsters keen to enjoy themselves. Clearly you must involve them in purposeful activity and hopefully you will follow the England Approach for the Nineties and begin with a warm-up followed by handling the ball.

Most writers on the game tend to eulogize when they talk about the French. They describe the French as having 'flair' and do so in a manner which suggests it's God-given and quite uncoachable. Nothing could be further from the truth. Those magically quick hands and that incisive running, which can cut great swathes in even the best of defences, are actually carefully thought out and practised.

Temperamentally the French like the ball in their hands and find the chore of winning it quite irksome. This is why when playing against the French any opponent with even the vaguest chance of winning has to stop the French at source. The rugby ball is their oxygen, without it they are mere mortals left gasping for breath, which brings me to their analysis of the English. They see us as being excellent at organization, that is, organizing the winning of the ball at scrums, line-outs, kick-offs and restarts. However, having won the ball they consider us to be very poor at 'liberating' it. Well, we are slowly getting better at this vital phase of the game but I know exactly what they mean and much of this justifiable criticism is related directly to how we teach the game.

To the French we start at the wrong end. We used to begin by teaching the scrum, line-outs and contact. They have always begun by teaching handling and the movement of the ball. Only after a few years, by which time a considerable amount of ball awareness, manipulative skills and continuity drills have been acquired, do they introduce what they look upon as the static organizational features of the game, the scrum and line-out. This is one of the reasons why we in England have radically altered our approach to the teaching of the game and why we have caused such chagrin in the minds of Mini/Midi coaches.

The latter tend to see the short, plump youngster as destined to be a prop from seven years of age onwards. The tall ten-year-old is always a lock, the fast boy is always a wing. Yet someone like Jeff Probyn, the England prop, has also played full back and centre. Bill Beaumont, now of A *Question of Sport* fame, was a schoolboy full back before becoming an England Captain and lock forward.

I've even received letters from fathers who say, 'My seven-year-old is frustrated that there is no contact in the game at this age,' or, 'You (the RFU) are ruining the production of front-row forwards by not allowing them to scrum until nine years of age.'

All mind-blowing comments when you look at the totality of a young player's career.

In part it's this stereotyping which seems so grossly unfair to the young player, and which is so restrictive an approach to the acquisition of skill. All skills to all players is no idle cliché but a real need. However, without a concentrated effort at teaching and coaching the many handling skills demanded by the game it is quite impossible to develop continuity. Continuity gives the game its aimed for flow and only when you have players who can handle well do you raise the game on to any worthwhile level of achievement.

If you are wondering whatever happened to the word passing, do not be alarmed; it is a part of handling. Handling might be described as the collective noun for all the recognized types of pass, like basic, switch, loop, miss out, scrum half, etc.

But it also includes passes which it would be difficult to put a name to unless you were a basketball player. One of the big changes of emphasis in the last ten to fifteen years has been the swing away from talking purely in terms of the pass to this word handling, because, at the end of the day, how you get the ball from A to B is immaterial provided B receives it at a height and speed that he can cope with. However, if there were a golden rule in handling it must be 'carry the ball in two hands'.

Having watched a lot of Mini/Midi Rugby, this is the one feature that stands out like a sore thumb and is directly responsible in 90 per cent of cases for the play coming to an abrupt end when the ball carrier is tackled. As every coach

Illus. 2

worth his salt will tell you, 'A ball carried under one arm is inviting a tackle.'

Even in this photograph, with the player in full flight for the line and carrying the ball in two hands, he would do well to note the two covering defenders and his own player in support on his inside. Should it be necessary, the ball carrier must have the mental speed and vision to quickly take the ball inside to his supporting players.

I divide handling into two categories: one that I call 'general', because it is training the player to develop such a high level of skill that the ball becomes almost an extension of his hands and involves the ability to take the ball in any direction, at any speed and at any height; the other I call 'specific' handling, and here I am talking about the specific passes associated with Rugby Football which I listed earlier in this section.

Perhaps the most basic practice, because it has the profoundest impact on almost all movements in the game, is on page 68. However, it is not the exercise that you would introduce to a raw beginner. Remember the latter probably won't be able to catch the ball let alone choose the correct running line.

Fig. 6.2. Group X and Y each begin at the same time but of course they are running in opposite directions.

The object for each player in each group is to begin by running on an arc, but to have found a straight line parallel to the touch-line of the grid *before* receiving a pass which should be taken almost flat.

When each group of four have completed their movement they regroup. The Ys take up the X positions and vice versa.

This exercise replicates so many movements/actions in rugby where initially your movements are away from the pass or in support of the ball carrier and if you don't succeed in getting on to a straight line *before* receiving the ball, you or another player in your team will end up by running into touch.

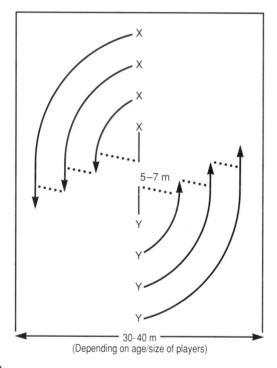

Fig. 6.2

In Fig. 6.3 the practice is replicated in a game situation and the player we are concentrating on is the full back (FB). The scrum half (S½) feeds the ball into the scrum. Meanwhile the full back runs as shown to take a flat pass from the scrum half.

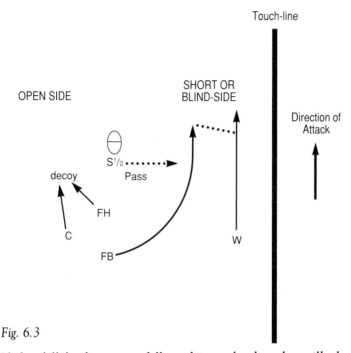

Fig. 6.3

If the full back cannot follow this angle then he will almost certainly either run into touch or restrict the available space for his wing (W). In either case the defence will have no difficulty in stopping the full back.

(1)   Please note that the fly half should make a decoy movement to the open side to distract the defence.

(2)   The teacher/coach *must* always make the connection between the practice that he has chosen and the game situation. It is my experience that very few players automatically see the relevance of the practice to the game. That doesn't mean they are not enjoying the practice. What it does mean is that it is your responsibility to signpost everything you do otherwise you could end up as a very busy practice organizer but a puzzled and frustrated coach.

For those Mini/Midi helpers whose knowledge of the game is not very great but who have played basketball, hockey, soccer or volleyball to a reasonable level, they need only remember some of the training games they play in these particular sports, and substitute the rugby ball. They will be pleasantly surprised how many small games they really do know. Let us look at two general handling activities.

PASSING ROUND THE SIDES OF A GRID

Note: A grid 10 metres square will be too large for seven-year-old boys, therefore make sure you adjust the size of the grids accordingly – this is where the plastic cones prove their versatility.

The reason for the boys facing outwards is to encourage them to reach to the side for the ball and then to swing it across their body.

Many developments are possible from this simple start. For example:

(1)   After each pass do three sit-ups or three press-ups and then stand up ready to receive the ball again as it is passed around the square.

(2)   Once they have passed the ball they follow it and touch the grid lines and return to their starting point.

This is a very good practice for developing in the minds of young players an awareness that once they have passed the ball they must follow it in order to provide support for the new ball carrier.

(3)   Introduce specific passes, for example, scrum half dive pass, or the sweep pass. It is optional, at this stage, whether or not you ask each player to follow their pass.

What you have to decide is whether you are concentrating on teaching good technique or whether you are more interested in their following the ball to develop their awareness of support and, as a by-product, improving their level of running fitness. If it's the former then you would be unwise to ask them to run

Illus. 3

Illus. 4 and 5

after their pass because fatigue will set in much quicker and when that happens skilled performance plummets.

Again, the purpose of this second general handling game (see Fig. 6.4) is to persuade young players to work together, to use their eyes and not to stand still calling for the ball (common fault), but to run into a space and thus give the ball carrier options.

The game begins with the ball carrier X1. At this moment X1 has no option other than to attempt to pass the ball to X2 because the rules of the game insist that the ball is passed only round the sides or edges of the grid. The onus is on X3 to move into the empty corner so that X1 now has an option of passing to either X2 or X3. If Y intercepts then he takes the place of the player who last passed the ball. Sometimes the Xs are so good or Y so poor that the same interceptor finds himself in the middle. Either be aware of this and see that all players take a turn at being interceptor or become very strict on the accuracy of the passing. For example, if the ball is dropped by an X, even if it is recovered, or if the ball goes out of the grid, then call this a mistake and make the player who made the mistake become the interceptor.

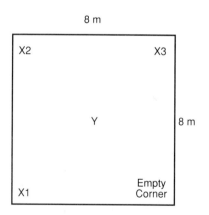

Fig. 6.4

For further ideas on grid games you should purchase the following publications from the RFU Shop at Twickenham:

Start Rugby (80 cards)
Skills Practices for All (Preliminary Award Booklet)
Even Better Rugby
A Selection of Skill Practices

THE BASIC PASS TO 'DRAW A MAN' OR 'FIX' AN OPPONENT

This is such an important skill that you simply cannot over-practise it. All players will be called upon to 'draw a man' or 'fix' an opponent at some time or other in a match, and the coach who assiduously makes his players practise this at every session will be rewarded handsomely. So many tries are thrown away through the ball carrier either passing the ball too early or too late. In making these comments, I am also consciously including international players who, believe it or not, are just as likely to have the same one-sidedness as the beginner. You see, most people are right-handed, therefore passing from right to left is usually far easier than from left to right. The Mini Rugby helper must therefore ensure that he sets up practices which encourage players to be technically proficient on either side of their body.

The description 'draw a man' is pure English. The description 'fix an opponent' is pure French. Nowadays I favour the latter because I believe it implies that an opponent is rooted to the spot whereas to draw a man is to bring one opponent towards the ball carrier. Perhaps some will feel it's a case of 'splitting hairs' but if the movements of the ball carrier can 'fix' or root an opponent then the next receiver of the ball will have much more time and space to make a decision.

Normally you fix an opponent by turning your shoulders inwards towards him thus causing him to hesitate and quite often actually stop. Fixing an opponent can be achieved some metres away from the ball carrier.

As always you should progress from static to passive to active opposition. Points to look for in this particular practice (see Fig. 6.5): the ball carrier X1 must engage the defending

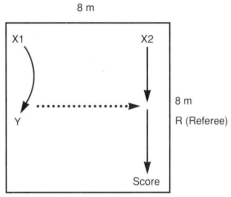

Fig. 6.5

player Y with his eyes and run at him. When he is sure that the defending player has been 'fixed' he turns his shoulders and head to his left, swings his arms and puts the ball out in front of X2. In the learning stage I always put the onus on X2 to be behind X1 because the latter usually has enough problems in fixing his opposite number and releasing the ball without worrying whether or not X2 will be in front of or behind him when he turns to release the pass. Once X1 has had a few turns then players rotate as follows: X1 takes the place of X2, X2 takes the place of R, R takes the place of Y, and Y now becomes the player who is practising fixing an opponent. Remember to set this practice up so that everyone also gets a chance to pass from left to right. (You will note I have included a player to act as referee and to look for the forward pass.)

The next progression is shown in Fig. 6.6 and Illus. 6 and 7. The referee is now one of the X players.

Player X1 has the ball in his hands and as soon as he moves his feet the activity begins. Y will move directly to X2 and try and catch him in possession of the ball. This means that X1 must ball the ball early enough so that X2 receives it with enough time to draw or fix Y before sending the ball out to X3.

Once all players have had a turn, then allow the defending player to go for either X2 or X3. If X2 has really understood his job then there is no way that Y should stop a try being scored

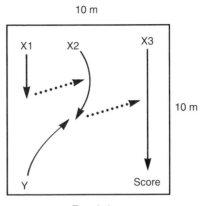

10 m

10 m

Fig. 6.6

Illus. 6 and 7

over the grid line because if Y is out of position then X2 will sell him a dummy and score himself.

Ask the players the following question: when can X2 reasonably expect to sell Y a dummy? Answer: only when X2 finds that Y is in front of him, or even better, on his way towards X3. Obviously, the golden rule for any defending player is always to keep on the inside of the ball carrier so that he has only one way to go (that is, usually the touch-line).

THE BASIC PASS TO 'TRANSFER THE BALL QUICKLY'

This is where a demonstration is absolutely essential because if you are intent on transferring the ball quickly you have to reach out to the side of your body and take the ball early on (see Illus. 8). With youngsters I have always found it best to position them either in front or behind the demonstrator but never at the side. Once the players have a mental picture of what you are asking them to do then you can make reasonably rapid progress.

Fig. 6.7. The ball begins with Y1. X1 and X2 are simply moving up and down the grid. When X1 is nearly level with Y1, then the latter gives him a pass. X1 takes it early, swings his arms and immediately puts it out in front of his partner X2. When X2 is level with Y2 he then passes him the ball.

Illus. 8

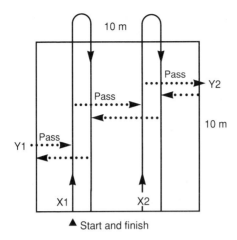

Fig. 6.7

On the return journey, it is now Y2 who gives it to X2 who has to take the ball early, swing his arms and immediately put the ball out in front of his partner X1. You will realize in this practice that only one player in turn transfers the ball quickly.

After a few lengths the Xs change over with the Ys. Of course, there is nothing to stop you having three runners – that is your choice. Only you know the capability of the players.

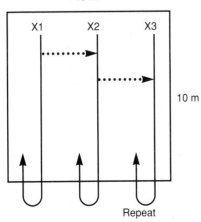

Fig. 6.8

Fig. 6.8 Virtually the same practice as above. X1 starts with the ball which travels to X2 and on to X3. Once X3 has reached the end of the grid, the activity is repeated. The practice is essentially for the middle player.

If you want to put more pressure on his ability to transfer the ball quickly then give all three players a smaller area to work in, or make them turn as soon as the ball reaches the end player.

Fig. 6.9 Same starting positions, but this time as soon as X1 has passed the ball he follows behind X2 and tries to put two hands on the shorts of X3 before the latter scores over the try line. This practice makes the ball really hum along the line.

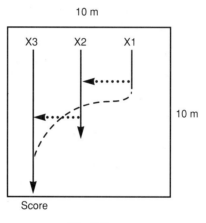

Fig. 6.9

The black-shirted players each have a ball (see Illus. 9) and act as scrum halves. The object of this practice is for the receivers to run straight and transfer the ball quickly (Illus. 10).

They have to remember that as soon as they have passed one ball another will be on its way, so their concentration must be absolute.

Once the end player has received a ball he puts it on the ground (with downward pressure – do not allow him to drop it or throw it away). Each scrum half follows the path of

Illus. 9 and 10

his own ball and goes to recover it, realigning himself exactly opposite the position he started (Fig. 6.10) because once all the balls have been placed on the ground the blacks will stop, turn around, realign and start back again. This means they will be passing off their right hands all the time so once you are happy with their skill level, I suggest you either start with the receivers on the other side of the scrum halfs or make the scrum halfs do more running by asking them to gather their own ball and sprint back to their original starting position. Do not forget the players must be equally competent passing off either hand.

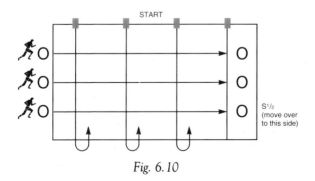

Fig. 6.10

PASS AND LOOP

The object of this is to create an extra pair of hands without increasing the number of players. In a normal three versus three (Fig. 6.11) the only likely outcome is stalemate but, because X1 is able to loop round X2, X1 will receive the ball again and be faced with either Y3 or, if Y3 sticks to his opposite number X3, then it should be possible for X1 to go through the gap between Y2 and Y3.

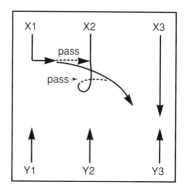

Fig. 6.11

THE SWITCH PASS

The switch pass is included here because it is such a useful means of either changing the direction of play or of keeping the movement going forward. For instance, a player is running out of space, perhaps a centre being forced towards the touch-line. The alert wing will realize what is happening and come inside taking the switch pass, thus keeping the movement going forward.

The starting positions of the four players are obvious. The ball carrier is Y1 and the other runner is Y2. Fig. 6.12 shows that Y1 must always turn the ball in the direction of the player who is going to take it out of his hands, in this case Y2. Why? Answer: because the receiver will always have the ball in his vision and for a split second the opposition will not.

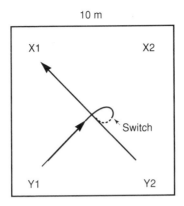

Fig. 6.12

The first ball carrier, that is the man switching the ball towards his partner, should not lose forward speed. This is a common fault amongst beginners. The ball carrier should only think of turning the top half of his body so allowing his legs to continue their forward motion.

The next progression is shown on page 82, see Illustration 11.

The front defender stands perfectly still. His partner behind him has to guess which side the switch will take place and put two hands on the shorts of the player he thinks has the ball. The ball carrier runs and when in front of the stationary player either performs the switch or dummy switch with his partner (see Illus. 12).

This very enjoyable practice ends the technique stage and so the scene is set for practising the switch against 'live' opposition. It is also time to introduce more realistic running lines for the players attempting the switch.

Obviously, a larger area is required for this three versus two practice (Fig. 6.13). X1 starts with the ball which he must give as soon as possible to X2 because the latter is being marked by Y1 (Fig. 6.14). For a very brief moment X2 will run at Y1, then away as hard as he can. In the meanwhile, X3 must run in his normal alignment so as to interest his opposite number Y2. If, for example, he were to move too early in the direction of X2 to attempt the switch then he would undoubtedly give Y2 time

Illus. 11 and 12

Starting positions
for 3v2   START
                         ▼

X3	X2	X1
		Ball
Y2	Y1	

15 m

Fig. 6.13

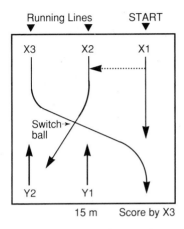

Fig. 6.14

to follow him. The message for X3 is very simple – leave the attempted switch as late as possible. Again, if you set this up as a demonstration, make certain that those watching do so from the ends so that they have a clear view of the running lines of X2 and X3.

I have no doubt whatsoever that you cannot over-emphasize the need for good handling skills and therefore even your warm-up should include ball skills as well as the more obvious stretching exercises. Again, I favour more young players being introduced to rugby through non-contact small-sided games because I have no doubt that the overall standard of performance would improve quite dramatically as those players moved on and upwards into the senior game.

7

BEATING AN OPPONENT

Perhaps the side-step and swerve are the two most exhilarating techniques to learn and eventually master so that a player can add them to his repertoire of skills, yet it was not so long ago they were generally considered to be the preserve of the few, and especially Welsh outside halves. Yet these techniques can be taught just as easily as all other techniques. The difficulty is not how to teach them but when to perform them in the game. A side which contains players who can side-step or swerve presents enormous problems for its opponents. These problems are magnified twofold if, for example, you find yourself faced with an opponent who can side-step off either foot. This is rare because normally a side-step is inside a covering defender and, as most people are right-footed, the majority of side-steppers do so from right to left.

Armed with this information you at least have some chance of stopping the runners. On the other hand, the player who possesses a swerve, which it must be admitted is really only possible for those who have the ability to change up a gear, will normally go on the outside of a defending player.

The following practice is one of the best I know for encouraging a player to beat an opponent by either of these methods and, at the same time, it offers the defending player an opportunity of learning how best to approach such a player so as not to be beaten – in other words, it is highly competitive.

Fig. 7.1 (overleaf) XI is the ball carrier and he begins by running towards Y1, draws him and passes to X2. As soon as X1 has passed, the teacher/coach taps Y2 on the shoulder, which is the latter's cue to move and try and put two hands on the shorts of X2 before he can score. X2, in the meanwhile, will be attempting to beat Y2 by side-step or swerve. The running lines of X2 are crucial and this is why the rest of the group have been so positioned.

For example, X2 can only hope to swerve outside Y2 if (a) he has a change of pace, or (b) he can persuade Y2 that he (X2) is either coming on his inside or at least going straight.

The photographs on page 87 show this practice in action.

Therefore, X2 must suggest to Y2 that he is interested

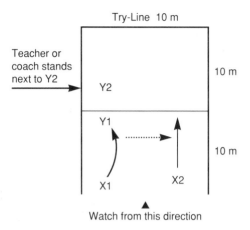

Fig. 7.1

in coming inside and this can be done by looking inside or straightening his run. Once X2 has persuaded Y2 to slow down that is the moment he must accelerate smartly away on the outside. This is also the moment he may transfer the ball from two hands to under the outside or right arm and, if necessary, be prepared to hand off Y2 with his left hand. (*Note:* there is no hand off or fend off allowed in the England version of Mini or Midi Rugby.)

Illus. 13

Illus. 14

Illus. 15 and 16

Now, if X2 wants to beat Y2 by side-step then almost the opposite happens. He should persuade Y2 that he intends to go on the outside and very slightly slow down in order to check his forward speed. By bending the right knee slightly and taking the weight on the right foot he is now ready to drive off again inside the covering player Y2.

Of course, if Y2 comes too quickly and X2 finds that Y2 is either straight in front of him or, even better, slightly on his outside (right), then this makes the side-step by X2 so much easier to execute. When the player X2 knows that he might be tackled, it is amazing how the survival faculty is sharpened and evasive action is taken!

The progressions I use are as follows:

(1)   As soon as X1 moves his feet then Y1 walks forward.

(2)   As soon as X1 moves his feet then Y1 runs forward.

(3)   The coach taps Y2 on the shoulder later on each/next occasion.

(4)   The coach varies the starting position of Y2 by moving him closer to the try line, as shown in Fig. 7.1.

(5)   When taking a large group and after everyone is familiar with the practice then the coach's services can be dispensed with. Y2 should only move when X1 has passed the ball.

(6)   After all these progressions have been tried with two hands on the shorts for a tackle, then repeat them with a proper tackle.

(7)   Switch the players round and ensure that whichever players are taking the role of Y1 and Y2 they start from the other side of the grid – this will ensure that players X1 and X2 develop their swerve and side-step skills off either foot.

8

CONFIDENCE IN CONTACT

What distinguishes rugby from most other games is that you can quite legitimately stop an opponent dead in their tracks, provided they are carrying the ball. For some players this is an enormous source of satisfaction. This blindingly obvious fact ought to be a stern reminder to the ball carrier that as there are opponents around who positively relish physical contact, it would be wise to get rid of the ball either before or immediately on contact and not to over-ambitiously run into the mouth of a concrete mixer.

Mick 'the Munch' Skinner (England) and Willie 'O' Ofahengaue (Australia) are but two players who have built their reputation on an ability to remove the oxygen, as well as the ball, from selfish ball carriers.

This is where over-enthusiastic adults often make horrendous mistakes when they teach young players. They arrive fresh from watching an international ready to impose adult standards on unsuspecting young players. For every youngster who likes contact I will name five who are put off initially by it and quickly leave the game. *Contact is all about confidence and confidence takes time to develop.* Sometimes over three or four seasons. Often the apparently natural and fearless tackler of tender years realizes, as they get older, that there are other actions that can be taken which are wiser and which will persuade the ball carrier to get rid of the ball without any need to tackle.

Certainly no-one in my schooldays ever suggested that they were going to teach contact, they always talked in terms of the tackle. Yet, when you watch any match it is patently obvious that there is much contact without there ever being a tackle. Over the last fifteen years the word contact has become the common noun for all aspects of the game where bodies collide and/or come into contact with the ground – in other words, tackling is only one part of contact.

For the very beginner it is almost certain that *the ground is the hardest object they will meet* and, therefore, learning how to fall is so important. I have said previously that I found relays to be a marvellously enjoyable way of involving a group of seven-year-olds and, of course, in these relays I always included forward rolls, sideways rolls, diving to score a try, etc. Naturally, I was aware that no rugby player would be expected to perform a roll of any description whilst playing the game, but equally I was conscious that they needed to know how to control themselves in a fall or tackle.

Having quick and sure reactions is also an important aspect of playing rugby to a high standard and so falling to the ground with a ball, on to the knees, buttocks, back, etc., and immediately springing back on to the feet at the command of the coach is another simple activity that should be introduced to the beginner. Before formal tackling is taught, the coach should ensure that the players have enough upper-body strength to cope.

This need for upper-body strength is essentially twofold.

(1)   It is a well-known fact that in athletics, the arms lead or drive the legs. You can illustrate this to yourself if you go for a run and find your legs feeling heavy. By driving your arms you will, for a short time, pick up the speed of your legs before the dreaded 'lactic acid' builds up to such an extent that your brain tells you to stop. Again, look at all world-class sprinters and note their upper-body development – it's not an accident or time misspent.

(2)   Upper-body strength is protection. You will never hang on to the ball in a tackle, or stop the ball carrier, if you have weak hands and arms. You will never rip the ball from an opponent if your upper body is weak. A common sight on the Mini Rugby pitch is to see the beginner trying to stop the ball carrier by groping round his neck and shoulders.

This is one reason why we in England have banned the hand off or fend off throughout the Mini/Midi age groups. In fact, it only becomes part of the game when the fifteen-a-side version is introduced at Under Thirteen level. The hand off or fend off is normally the preserve of the big boy who tucks the ball under one arm and ploughs his way to the opponent's goal line scattering nervous children aside like confetti.

Apart from the fact that tackling round the neck is dangerous and illegal, rarely is it effective. No-one can run with their legs firmly wrapped together and that still remains for most young players the most effective and safe tackle.

Many Mini Rugby coaches will recall their own playing days and particularly at the beginning of the season if the grounds were hard, when the first contact with the ground removed skin from the knees, hips, and elbows and left them feeling distinctly groggy, and when going into the scrum for the first time was like being cast into a concrete mixer. Two games and the body of the experienced player is attuned to the new season. The Mini/Midi Rugby player cannot possibly adjust that quickly in spite of the resilience of youth because he does not possess the skills which make a speedy adjustment possible. These and many other factors demand that due care and attention is paid to increasing gradually the quantity and intensity of contact work through competitive strengthening exercises and then teaching the correct techniques of the side, rear and front tackles.

Without doubt the best book on this subject is *Even Better Rugby*, published by the Rugby Football Union. In *Even Better Rugby* twenty or thirty such activities are illustrated and the Mini Rugby coach is earnestly recommended to purchase a copy.

Here are a few examples:

Illus. 17: Wheelbarrow. Chinese Wrestling. Passive neck exercise.

As always with beginners, try to ensure that wherever possible boys and girls of the same size are partnered.

8.1 TACKLING

Remember, no-one can run with their legs together!

When teaching beginners it is recommended that tackling should be introduced on a soft surface and that the players should take their boots off and work in stocking feet or in training shoes.

After all, there is no point in running the risk of receiving a glancing blow from a boot when the prime object of the exercise is to generate confidence through the learning of correct techniques.

It should also be stressed that many coaches help young players to gain further confidence by flinging themselves at a tackling bag. This helps generate tremendous drive off the ground and into the tackle.

THE SIDE TACKLE

Illus. 18: Right shoulder into thigh. Head behind seat/shorts. Pull arms together as you drive from the ground. Do not intertwine your fingers.

See Illus. 19 (overleaf). The boy on the right moves forward on his knees and is tackled by the boy on the left.

Progression:

The tackler is now in the crouch position and the tackled player walks forward, as shown in Illus. 20, 21 and 22.

Illus. 19

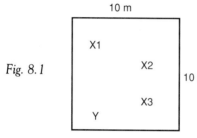

Fig. 8.1

In Fig. 8.1 Y is the tackler but all players are on their knees. Naturally the X players are moving round the grid trying to avoid being tackled by Y.

Illus. 20

Illus. 21 and 22

Progression:

Next introduce the ball because (a) you cannot tackle someone who does not have the ball and (b) the tackled player needs to learn how to keep possession on contact. In Fig. 8.2 you will see that the tackler Y is under much more pressure, for example –

(1)   How many side-tackles can Y make in 10 seconds, etc?

(2)   How many tries can the Xs score in 10 seconds, 20 seconds? Keep changing positions.

>   *Note:* Xs must progress from first a walk, to a jog and, finally, to a run. In all the progressions they must run in a straight line.

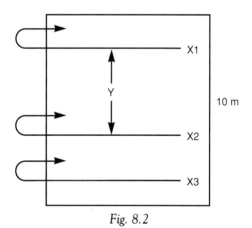

Fig. 8.2

THE FRONT TACKLE

In many ways I always find this the easiest to teach because the tackler uses the weight of the ball carrier to bring the latter down. All the tackler has to say to himself is, I must sit, fall backwards and TURN so that I end up on top. Start in CROUCH position (Illus. 23, 24 and 25).

Full marks to the tackler and to the tackled player in Illus. 26, especially as the latter has kept possession of the ball. The coach should ask the tackled player to walk alternately to the left then right shoulder of the tackler.

Illus. 23 and 24

Illus. 25 and 26

Progression:

(1)   Fig. 8.3. Y should remember to sit, fall backwards and
        turn to land on top in each tackle.

10 m

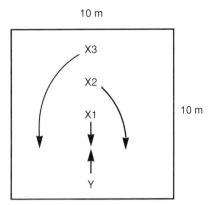

10 m

Fig. 8.3

(2)   As soon as Y has tackled X1 then X2 runs to the other side of Y so that not only does Y have to tackle but he has to pick himself off the ground and quickly get into position to take X2.

(3)   Once he has tackled X2 then X3 will be on his way.

REAR TACKLE

Wearing trainers is better than wearing boots when learing to tackle. In fact, with absolute beginners, as previously stated, it is recommended that tackling should be introduced in bare or stocking feet.

Illus. 27: Head either behind seat or to side, arms round thigh, squeeze tight and drive.

Progression:

(1)   Repeat, start as in Illus. 27 but both moving on knees.

(2)   Tackler starts in the crouch position with the player to be tackled some 5 metres behind him and carrying a ball.

Remember, now that there is a moving target, you must aim at the waist and allow your arms to slide down, squeezing as you slide until your arms can comfortably bring together the legs of the tackled player.

(3)   Both in sprint start position, see below. The back player is the tackler and he calls 'go'. On this command, the front boy sprints to pick up the ball and score over the grid line. The back man may tackle his partner either before or after he has picked up the ball.

Illus. 28 and 29

Illus. 30

All these tackles, side, front, and rear, can be attempted in competitive three versus one games in the grids. For example, one player is the tackler and the other three carry a ball as they walk anywhere they like in the grid to avoid the tackle. Because the tackler can run, he does have an advantage. Once a player is tackled then they go out of the grid (make certain they stand well away from other grids). See how long it takes the tackler to bring the three players down. Each player takes their turn to be the tackler and the time that it takes is recorded. The coach should note the times because these can be quite an incentive to players to improve their tackling ability and, as a by-product, because the players are working under pressure their running fitness is considerably increased.

In many respects the techniques of the various tackles are very simple to teach – the major problem is still to follow. Being able to tackle implies being in the correct position and this factor, more than any, separates the sheep from the goats. So many players, at all levels, are beaten not because they do not understand how to tackle or because they lack courage, but because they do not know how to put themselves in the best position in order to tackle.

Therefore, it is essential to show the players how to 'line-up' the ball carrier so that he has little chance to escape the tackler's clutches. Basically, you keep on the in-field side of the ball carrier, forcing him outwards towards the touch-line – this at least ensures that he has only one direction to go.

You must get under their guard and aim for a point at least 1 metre the other side of them (side tackle) so that when your shoulder makes contact with their thigh they are knocked off balance – your arms do the rest. If a player coming straight at you is 10 or 20 metres away, do not remain stationary. Move towards them at a controlled pace so that you not only cut down the physical distance but you cut down their thinking time.

You will be pleasantly surprised how often the initiative can be seized by this action.

Finally, you have to choose the correct tackle for the situation in which you find yourself and obviously this is particularly hard for the Mini Rugby player who, by virtue of his age, is bound to be inexperienced. In Illus. 31 and 32 a very commendable tackle has been made but, of course, the tackled player is still able to pass the ball.

Illus. 31 and 32

Either a more forceful tackle was required or a smother tackle in which the tackled player has his arms and the ball pinned to his body. Personally, I would let this type of tackle evolve not as a tackle *per se* but as part of the close-quarter work associated with mauls where a player throws the ball carrier to the ground.

8.2 CONTINUITY

The games which really flow and are enjoyable to play in or watch are dependent on good communications between forwards and backs, excellent handling from all players and the priceless ability to keep possession, especially the skill(s) needed to recycle the ball in contact.

The uninterrupted connection between forwards and backs is not easy to achieve. Not only are opponents highly motivated to break the chain but any lack of skill or misjudgement by the team in possession is also certain to bring the play to a halt. This is why, once contact has been introduced to youngsters, they need to know about body position, how to 'lift' a stationary ball close to the tackled player and to 'pick up' the rolling ball or the ball which is in open play without losing speed. They also need to be taught the rudiments of the ruck and maul.

Much has been written about the ruck and maul over the years but I still incline to the New Zealand approach that it is better to teach the ruck before the maul because although both require forward drive to be successful, it is in the ruck that you can more easily generate this quality. However, before looking at the respective techniques, I also hold firmly to a long-held view that, as a guiding principle, rucks and mauls are failures, that is *failures to keep the ball moving forward*. If the coach really works hard on the first two principles of play, that is, Go *Forward* and *Support*, then rarely will it be necessary to ruck or maul and especially is this true of Mini/Midi Rugby. Therefore, this is where the emphasis should be placed and just to remind you of what was said earlier,

(1)   If the ball is on the ground in front of you then

pick it up and drive forward. Support must be close to, and directly behind the ball carrier and not spread out laterally with players screaming for the ball.

(2)   If the tackled player has placed the ball close to their body, then step over that player, bend your knees to lower your centre of gravity and lift up the ball – this will keep you in a very strong and safe position. See Illus. 33 and 34.

(3)   If the ball is on the ground but behind you, fall on it by getting alongside the ball, putting your body between the ball and the opposition, securing the ball with one or both hands and then standing up immediately.

These skills must be taught as priorities as soon as the contact stage is approaching and one of the simples ways is through team relays.

8.3 THE RUCK

Let me stress at this point that there is no question of introducing the formal ruck – the whole emphasis is geared to the players being able to keep the ball moving forward for as long as possible. If they can go round players all well and good! Only when they are finally checked do they need to be able to either ruck or maul the ball back, depending on the circumstances. When they have reached the stage of being stopped by an opponent then they can either feed or pass the ball to a supporting player who, in turn, will either drive forward or perhaps set up a maul, or the player first stopped will have been taught to put the ball on the ground behind him so that it can be seen by the forwards – this is their cue to drive over the ball in a ruck formation.

All coaches have their turn of phrase so that the players can better imagine what is required. One well-known New Zealand coach of past vintage was especially forthright. So many players go into rucks as though they are straining to see over a nudist's fence. As a result, he had all the players screaming the word 'socks'. The idea sounds crazy, but it worked. It is frustrating beyond words for any coach to see the ball being kicked forward in the ruck by unthinking players who have their head in the clouds. With your eyes on the 'socks' this cannot happen (hopefully!).

The stage has now been reached when opposition is required. Again, take four players working over two grids (10 m × 20 m). Number 1 runs forward, falls with his back/waist so that it can be seen by his own players. Number 2 puts a foot over Number 1, lifts up the ball and drives on. The ball carrier then slips the ball to Number 3 and becomes the oppositin by turning to face Number 3. Number 3 drives into Number 2 and slides to the ground, putting his body between the ball and Number 2 or slips the ball to the ground between his legs and stays on his feet.

his legs and stays on his feet.

In the meanwhile, Number 4 has followed the action and now puts a foot over Number 3 and/or picks up and slips the ball to Number 1, who is now back on his feet and up in support. Number 1 goes over the end of the grid to score. Player Number 1 starts, and ends, by scoring – a very simple practice.

At this stage, you will, of course, be talking and dem-

Illus. 33

Illus. 34

onstrating how contact is made. The ball carrier should try and put the defending player off balance and aim to come up under his guard (just beneath the front ribs). Naturally, the ball should be carried firmly in two hands and held close to the body on contact yet as far away from the opponent as the ball carrier's shape and size will allow. The greatest failing at this point is either the players are so enthusiastic about making contact that they positively launch themselves at opponents and everyone ends up on the ground, or a player does not relish the contact and turns his body before reaching an opponent so that all forward momentum is lost.

This is why all players, even internationals, need to generate forward drive which can only be achieved by 'pumping the legs hard'.

Principles are principles in any language and a fundamental truth of making progress towards an opponent's line, if there is a body in the way, is that you must lead with the shoulders, drive with the legs and bind tightly with supporting players.

If there is a pattern to a mini ruck, and I am not absolutely certain one is necessary, then I would say it was to aim for a 1:2 formation for Mini Rugby and 1:2:1 with one standing out for Midi Rugby. See Illus. 35, 36 and 37. In other words, if the

Illus. 35 and 36 (below)

ball has not been picked up or has been deliberately placed on the ground, then a platform should already have been established for the first two supporting players to zero in on the rear end of the player from their side who must be on his feet. These two players will have bound on to themselves with their inside arm

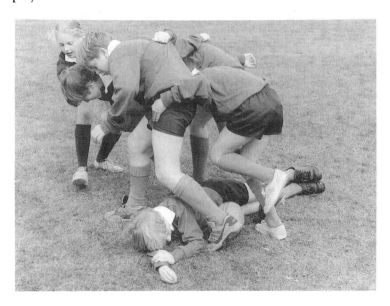

Illus. 37: Remember – lead with the shoulders, drive with the legs and bind tight with the arms.

and with their outside arm be grabbing shorts of any opponent on their side of the ruck. The other Mini Rugby forward will be putting his head between the buttocks of the two driving players in front of him thus helping to give maximum forward drive.

If there is any defending to be done at rucks, or mauls for that matter, then the scrum half would do well to look initially for danger down the short- or blind-side of the field.

8.4 THE MAUL

A large number of coaches do encourage the ruck but an equally large number are more inclined to the maul because, primarily, the ball is in the hands and, therefore, the scrum half can call for it when he feels the moment is right.

Devotees of the maul would also argue that it tends to be less physical than the ruck and for some children this is a much more gentle and acceptable introduction to such an important phase of the game.

Whatever the preference, the principles of the ruck apply equally to the maul. It is worth noting that whereas the law only requires two players for a ruck to be formed, that is, 'when the ball is on the ground and one or more players from each team are on their feet and in physical contact, closing around the ball between them', three players are required for a maul to be formed. That is, the man carrying the ball, another player from his team and one opponent. Again, there are many practices leading up to the mini maul and there are certainly two or three methods of mauling. Here are a few simple activities.

The idea is that Y1, the ball carrier, should run towards the stationary player X1 ready to present the ball to his supporting player Y2 who will score over the grid line (see Fig. 8.4).

10 m

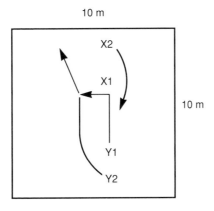

10 m

Fig. 8.4

As soon as Y1 is on his way then X2 may move forward to either the left or right of X1, without in any way interfering with either of the Y players. If X2 decides to move forward to the left of X1, as above, then Y1 must produce the ball on the right side of X1, Y2 must react quickly to ensure that he is on the correct side of Y1 to take the ball forward to score. The age, ability and experience of the players should be the deciding factor in how much contact is made initially between Y1 and X1. For example:

(1)   With absolute beginners Y1 may have the ball taken off him by Y2 before contact is made with X1.

(2)   As confidence grows, then Y2 should take the ball off Y1 after contact.

(3)   As soon as Y1 moves then X1 may walk towards him, etc.

Illus. 38

In Illus. 38, the ball carrier is driving into the head-banded defender making sure that he keeps the ball as far away from the defender as possible. He is also staying on his feet.

In the next, Illus. 39, the supporting player leads with the left or outside arm and drives into a teammate whilst, at the same time, securing the ball. In fact, the ball will soon be held between these two players.

In the meantime, another two supporting players have arrived (Illus. 40) and are aiming to bind over the back of the player you see holding the ball in Illus. 38 and 39. (*Note:* the boy on the right has his arm around the shoulder instead of around the back of the boy on the left.) With their outside arms they would try to bind on to opponents so as to ensure there were no stragglers round the fringes of this maul.

By now the first supporting player has taken the ball off his

Illus. 39 and 40

own player (the ball carrier in Illus. 38), and would be ready to present it to his scrum half. The scrum half, who is the 'eyes' of the forwards, would call for the ball when he thinks the time is right. This part of the operation is vitally important. Do not allow the forwards to deliver the ball from the mini maul when they feel like it – ensure that the scrum half dictates the time.

In any method of mauling there should be forward drive! Do not forget that if a team is going forward then the opposition must be on the retreat, and this makes life so much easier for the half backs of the team going forward.

Whatever method you choose, do not forget the principles: you will only go forward if you lead with the shoulders, drive with the legs and bind tightly with supporting players.

9

THE BACKS

The backs consist of a scrum half, fly half, two centres, two wings, and one full back in the fifteen-a-side game.

As so much effort should be expended on handling skills in the early teaching of the game, it follows that there is much merit in introducing next the concept of the backs as a unit. However, a word of caution is again called for.

With the six backs of Mini Rugby, that is, the scrum half, fly half, centre, two wings and full back and the seven backs of Midi Rugby (as with Mini but with two centres), you really do have to crawl before you walk. There is no way the game will take shape unless the handling skills are mastered. Perhaps for Mini Rugby players there is a strong case for unopposed rugby in the initial stages in order to have a clear mental picture of the patterns of the game, but the coach must nevertheless realize the real problem for any back is that if they are ever going to operate effectively in a game then at some time or another in the practice session they must be faced with opposition. In many respects, coaching of the backs should be a process of self-discovery. The coach is, in fact, the catalyst, setting up or creating match situations so that the backs provide their own answers with, of course, guidance from the coach. Backs in particular need to be mentally and physically challenged and it is quite useless to send them down to the other end of the field with a curt rejoinder: 'Off you go and practise a few moves.' The backs really do need and deserve your attention.

Sooner or later the backs as a unit are going to have to understand the practical significance and theory surrounding two imaginary lines which we call the gain line and the tackle line. This does not warrant a formal lecture from the coach, but it does mean that the coach should understand the theory and translate it into words which will be understood by whatever age group he is taking.

As shown in Fig. 9.1, we have a typical situation in any Mini Rugby game with, in this instance, team A ready to put the ball in the scrum. All being well, team A will gain quality possession of the ball and team B will come up on them as fast as possible to tackle and dispossess them of the ball. If they can, team A will cross the imaginary line, the gain line, before they are tackled – team B will be trying to make certain that they tackle and dispossess team A on team A's side of the gain line.

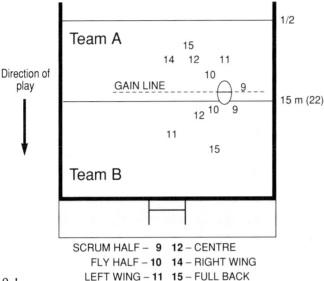

Fig. 9.1

SCRUM HALF – **9**   **12** – CENTRE
FLY HALF – **10**   **14** – RIGHT WING
LEFT WING – **11**   **15** – FULL BACK

Wherever the tackles do take place will be the second imaginary line, the tackle line, and trying to ensure that this line is on the other side of the gain line – in other words in front of your own forwards – is so important. If your backs are tackled behind their own forwards then the forwards will not thank you because they will have to run across the field and, what is worse, run towards their own goal line, before they can become onside and take part in the game again. In this illustration, if team A's forwards can pick their heads up from the scrum and run straight into the fray then they will do so with greater speed and purpose because there is no doubt that psychologically forwards do not enjoy pushing their guts out in a scrum only to find that their backs have made a mistake behind them. In plain English, get a ball carrier in front of your forwards.

The next question we should now ask ourselves is, how do we get a ball carrier in front of our forwards? There are obviously two simple ways:

(1)   By running and handling.

(2)   By kicking.

Not unnaturally, at Mini Rugby level it is on the former that the most attention should be placed for reasons previously given, and until you have found a pair of good half backs nothing else matters behind the scrum. It is no accident that half backs are the link between the forwards and the three-quarters and are largely responsible for giving the game its pattern.

Their responsibilities are onerous and for ease of under-standing I would recommend you find and read a very old booklet called *The ABC of Rugby* (1960) by C.K. Saxton, a former All Black, in which he talks about the three Ps. They are Possession, Position and Pace and, if related to the backs, they really do make you think. *They basically cover how a ball carrier gets in front of the forwards.*

9.1 GETTING A BALL CARRIER IN FRONT OF THE FORWARDS BY:
Running and Handling

POSSESSION

(1)   All backs, and half backs in particular, must recognize the type of possession they are given and use it effectively. Clearly a ball from the scrum slowly delivered restricts your attacking possibilities, yet so many backs at all levels have been guilty of calling a move long before they have received the ball. They have then proceeded to carry out the predetermined move even when the ball they were given by the forwards was accompanied by opposition back-row scavengers or when, if they had only used their eyes, they would have noticed that one of the opposition backs was hopelessly out of position and a different action was called for.

(2)   Do not squander the ball you have been given – remem-

ber, the forwards have sweated buckets of perspiration and they will not take kindly, for example, to someone kicking it straight down the opposition full back's throat for the latter to look like a world-call player. Similarly, if a back is caught in possession of the ball he should be strong enough and technically accomplished to retain possession long enough for a colleague to support him and so allow his team to keep possession of the ball. As a back, you generally are the nearest player to the breakdown. Ten to fifteen years ago, no self-respecting back would have got himself involved in close three-quarter contact or be seen wrestling for the ball – these actions were strictly for the forwards. Today, if the centre passes to the wing the nearest supporting player may well be the passer of the ball and, therefore, if he has been taught how to regain possession, that player should instantly follow the ball, wrench it off whoever has it and, if possible, keep the play going forward or set up a maul/ruck.

POSITION

The important question that all backs should ask themselves is, am I in the correct position to make use of the ball? One of the oldest and simplest guidelines is for a player to see if he can read the number on the back of the shirt of the player on his inside. If he can, then he can't be lying flat! The other simple tip in order to help stop the natural outward drift of backs is to stand with his outside foot forward – give it a try.

However, the surest way of running straight is to have practised endlessly the simple drill in Chapter Six and then to have progressed against opposition.

The other questions which backs should ask themselves are:

How much space do players need if attacking through the wing, fly half, centre, full back?

Can we straighten the line? Why?

When do we run across the field? Why?

How do we create space for ourselves and others?

What makes an effective switch, loop?

How can passing create space?

Should a player always be 'drawn' or 'fixed'?

Can you score off every overlap you create?

Can you put a player into a gap?

The third P is . . .

PACE

That is: speed of ball, speed of running, speed of thought.

Imagine if Linford Christie or Roger Black, our Olympic runners, played rugby – they would certainly take some stopping! Yet there is no doubt that the ball passed at the correct height between sure handlers will travel much faster than even Linford or Roger. Also, players who are not blessed with great natural speed over the ground can more than compensate for this comparative deficiency by being able to think quickly. Perhaps Will Carling's and Jeremy Guscott's most priceless asset on the rugby field is not their running speed but their thinking speed. More often than not they anticipate their opponents' defence and, as a result, they are able to put themselves into a space between the centres or centre and wings. They can make it look deceptively easy.

One of the simplest and best practices for the backs who have had at least two seasons' Mini Rugby is for the coach to walk along the 15-metre line (Fig. 9.2) carrying a ball with his six attacking backs aligned ready to move the ball at whatever moment the coach decides to give it to the scrum half: the coach is in essence a walking scrum. Clearly, as the coach walks towards the middle of the 15-metre line then the field splits for the attacking backs – this is something the coach will have to point out initially but the players will soon learn this for themselves. When the field splits, the centre, one wing and fly half will be on one side of the scrum and the other wing on the other side, or vice versa, depending on which way the fly half elects to run the ball. At this stage, the attacking side full back is free to join the backs in front of him. The object of the exercise is to move the ball without introducing miss-outs, loops, switches, etc., because the opposition will usually begin with two players whose only task is to put two hands on the shorts of whoever has the ball. Do not be surprised if the two-man defence wins every time in the early stages!

As the attackers become more competent, then gradually introduce another defender and give the defence specific players to mark so that maybe the only two players unmarked on the attacking side are the full back and one wing. The onus on the attackers now is to see how they can bring these two unmarked players into the action.

This practice is very useful for the inexperienced defender as well, because they learn to keep a close eye on their opposite number and when the field splits – scrum centre of 15-metre (22 m) line – they soon realize that they must not allow themselves to become confused and thus fail to mark their man. Once you have developed this practice to full opposition, then allow the scrum half to make a break. If all is proceeding well, give each team a name, for example A and B, and call out whichever side is going to receive the ball some three seconds before you actually give it to the respective scrum half.

This ensures that not only will both sides get their turn but they will have to quickly realign.

Once you are satisfied that the players understand the practice, that they can really move the ball quickly and are able to score tries, then the coach might try walking at diagonals instead of along the 15-metre (22 m) line (see Fig. 9.2). This means that defenders now have to realign and defend from a retreating position, which is precisely what they will have to do in the Mini Rugby game.

Incidentally, in these practices I strongly recommend that the coach insists that the scrum half should develop the ability to pass off either hand and so if he is passing to the left it's off his right hand, and if he is passing to his right it's off his

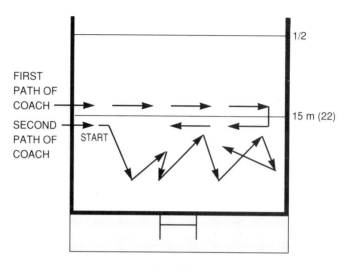

Fig. 9.2

left hand. This may be awkward for the scrum half for a long while but rest assured that the players will thank you in a few years' time! Do not forget that when the scrum half is playing the fifteen-a-side game there is nothing more satisfying to his opposite number, or some mean-minded flank forward, than to realize that they have the pleasure of marking a one-sided scrum half!

A coach should never hesitate to repeat a practice in order to make sure that it has been understood. It is during extra practice that the coach has time to focus his attention on other individual faults.

Note: The coach would be advised to begin by passing the easy way, that is from right to left.

The running lines of the fly half (FH), centre (C) and wing (W) in defence are no different from the full game, namely, these three players should aim to approach their opposite numbers so that they push them outwards towards the touch-line (see Fig. 9.3). As we saw with the 'drawing' or 'fixing' practice in grids, it's the easiest thing in the world for the ball carrier to

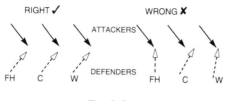

Fig. 9.3

sell a dummy if the defending player is either square on to the ball carrier or on his outside.

What happens if the opposition full back enters the back line? The following are possible solutions.

(1)   Your own full back comes up and takes his opposite number leaving your own wing to look after his man.

(2)   The wing steps in and takes the full back leaving your own full back to take the attacking wing (see Fig. 9.4).

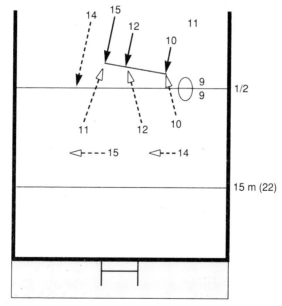

Fig. 9.4: Choice (2). The defending wing No. 11 steps in and takes the full back No. 15.

(3)   The backs 'drift' out one position. In other words, from, say, a scrum ball 10 metres off the touch-line, where you suspect the opposition will bring in their full back, and, therefore, it is fairly certain that the ball will have to move instantly through the hands of the attacking team's fly half having checked that his opposite number has definitely passed the ball and can move out one place and mark the centre. The defending team's centre then takes the extra man (full back) and wing takes wing.

It has to be admitted that, of the three choices given above, (2) is the one that I would recommend because when the attacking team's full back is receiving the ball he is bound to be looking inside to his centre and, even if the defending wing is not quick enough to catch the full back in possession, it is going to take a very good attacking full back to cope with a wing coming in at him from an angle and still be able to pass the ball to his wing. Besides in the Mini game you still have another wing 14 covering.

In this very brief look at the running and handling aspects of back play one overriding point has to be stressed and that concerns attitude. You do not produce runners and handlers of the ball unless they do this every week. The coach should cultivate this attitude.

Finally, as a piece of potted wisdom, I commend to you the advice of W.D. Gibbon who, in 1922, wrote:

The first duty of
    a scrum – is to get the ball
    a scrum half – is to pass
    a fly half – is to get his three-quarters on the move
    a centre three-quarter – is to make openings for his wing
    a wing three-quarter – is to run
    a full back – is to be in the right place.

The secret of
    successful passing – is to give and take passes on the move
    sustained passing – is to back up on the open side

successful backing up – is to keep on your feet
try-getting – is to keep the ball out of touch
getting the ball in the scrum – is to get the first shove
successful defence – is to go for the man with the ball
successful tackling – is to throw yourself at the man with the ball.

9.2 GETTING A BALL CARRIER IN FRONT OF THE FORWARDS BY:
Kicking

As a broad understanding of the game is developed a winning way evolves. However, in this evolutionary process one inescapable conclusion is reached and it is that kicking the ball out of the hand plays a significant part in the tactics of the game. (Remember kicking is introduced at Under Eleven in the Mini game in England.)

It's also an inescapable conclusion that any team without a goal-kicker will struggle.

If you watch any group of youngsters playing with a rugby ball in their own time, more often than not they will be kicking it rather than running and passing. Perhaps it's because the majority are saturated through television with the round ball game where kicking is the only choice. Whatever reason it wouldn't be so bad if their kicking practice was structured (with the proviso stated on page 28 in relation to the beginner) and had a purpose but sadly this is rarely the case.

Teachers and coaches would do well to introduce youngsters to the RFU Proficiency Award, as Test 5 specifically looks for accuracy in both kicking and catching the ball in well-defined grids or channels (see Fig. 9.5 overleaf).

The following are the essential points of the different kicking techniques.

PUNT

Used as a defensive measure to relieve pressure or to gain ground from a free kick or penalty, or as an attacking move by kicking into effective areas.

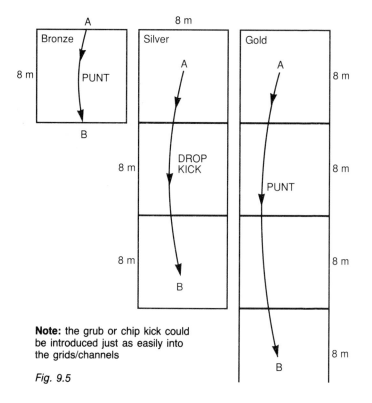

Note: the grub or chip kick could be introduced just as easily into the grids/channels

Fig. 9.5

ESSENTIALS OF TECHNIQUE

(1)   Keep your eyes on the ball at all times.

(2)   The ball should be held at the angle it should be placed on the foot.

    In Illus. 41 the kicker is kicking with his right foot to the left touch. By slightly angling the ball towards the touch-line the ball will screw (spin round its long axis) in that direction when kicked.

(3)   See how the ball fits on to the laced part of the boot (Illus. 42).

(4)   Try to get a good 'follow-through'. The ball will go in the direction you kick it so ensure that your leg swings through the ball towards the target.

Illus. 41 and 42

DROP KICK

Used when kicking for height or distance as when restarting play (kick-off) or when trying for a drop goal in open play.

ESSENTIALS OF TECHNIQUE)

(1)   Watch the ball all the time.
(2)   Drop the ball so that when it rebounds from the

Illus. 43 and 44

ground it is at such an angle that it will fit the instep
of your foot.

(3)   Kick through the ball as in the punt.

GRUB KICK

Used as an attacking move to put the ball behind defenders
and in front of your colleagues. This type of kick is used mainly
by backs to breach a shallow lying defence as an alternative to a
short punt. However, it is important that there is a gap through

Illus. 45

which the ball can be sent, otherwise the ball merely strikes the feet of the defenders and rebounds behind your backs!

Or used as a kick-off, particularly in wet weather to force opponents into knocking on a difficult bouncing ball.

ESSENTIALS OF TECHNIQUE (Illus. 45)

(1)   Watch the ball all the time.

(2)   Drop the ball so that it fits the angle of the instep after rebounding from the ground.

(3)   Try to kick the ball along the ground. The ankle is extended but the leg is not completely straightened.

(4)   The follow through indicates how the knee tends to lead throughout the kick. As an alternative, send the ball along the ground by using the side of the foot.

CHIP KICK

Generally used as an attacking ploy, especially when faced with a three-quarter line who are lying flat. This kick requires accuracy in its execution over the heads of the advancing three-quarters, and speed in the follow up to catch the ball. It is also very effective when confronted by a group of stationary forwards who may find it extremely difficult to turn quickly enough.

Illus. 46 and 47

ESSENTIALS OF TECHNIQUE

(1)   As height is required quickly, the kicking leg needs to be well bent at the knee.

(2)   This action will help the ball to rise quickly over the advancing players.

(3)   The kicker must move rapidly through a gap to pursue the ball.

PLACE KICK

Used as a penalty kick or to start the game.

Illus. 48 and 49

ESSENTIALS OF TECHNIQUE

(1)   Watch the ball all the time.

(2)   Accelerate throughout the approach. (Illus. 49.)

(3)   The non-kicking foot lands to the side but *behind* the ball. (Illus. 48.)

(4)   The ball is struck with the toe . . . this is an odd method used by the kicker who runs straight up to the ball . . . or the top of the foot (laces) and instep kicker who approaches from an angle.

(5)   Kick through the ball. (Illus. 50.)

The above skills are all perfectly simple and comparatively easy to do in isolation. You must, having mastered the actual techniques, practise them in game-like situations (including

Illus. 50

goal kicks) in order to produce the required movement when under physical and possibly mental pressure.

I cannot stress enough the use of cones as target areas so that youngsters not only develop a sound and trusting technique but they know:

(1)   Why they are kicking.

(2)   What type of kick is required.

(3)   Precisely where they are kicking (this is why the target of cones is essential) and who is chasing the kick.

Only then does the kicking practice become purposeful.

10

THE FORWARDS – THE BALL WINNERS

Experience leads me to the conclusion that no matter what has happened over the decades to the laws of the fifteen-a-side game, forwards win matches. Without the ball rugby is an impossible game – the odds are too heavily stacked against any team no matter how talented their backs. This statement now applies to Mini/Midi, although to a lesser degree. I have made it obvious from the very beginning of this book that it is the function of the forwards to win kick-offs/restarts, scrums, and line-outs. Their involvement in the game doesn't begin and end at that point because their ability to be up in support of whoever has the ball is crucial. However, if they cannot carry out their primary task they will certainly not be able to carry out their secondary role.

10.1 THE SCRUM

In England the passive scrum (no pushing) is first introduced to the Under Nines and by Under Ten the scrum is fully active. As I personally never saw a rugby ball until I was thirteen I am inclined to think that Under Nine is too young but I bow to the majority view. Regardless of the age of the youngsters let us not lose sight of the prime objective of the scrum and that is to ensure that the unit goes forward so that the hooker has the best chance of striking for and winning the ball. These skills have to be taught – they don't just happen. (Illus. 51.)

One of the least satisfying things to hear is that a total newcomer to rugby, of any age, is thrown straight into the active scrum at his first lesson. It is vital that certain principles are understood and taught with care.

Remember . . .

(1)   You cannot push if your legs are straight – you can only lock the scrum in this position – therefore drop your hips slightly towards the ground and bend your knees.

(2)   You cannot push effectively if you have a rounded back like a camel. See Illus. 51: no to round back, yes to flat back.

Illus. 51: Right pair: quite good driving position from boy on left, i.e., flat back, knees bent. Good locking position from boy on right because feet back, plenty of studs in contact with ground, knees braced to receive drive.

(3)   If your hips are higher than your shoulders then all your efforts will disappear into the ground. Not only is this ineffective but it will cause the scrum to collapse which is illegal and potentially dangerous.

(4)   Feet back – not under the hips/seat.

(5)   As much stud contact with the ground as possible – it is extremely difficult to scrummage on the toes although if the scrum is not steady then obviously players will be forced to scrummage on their toes in order to maintain their balance.

Using a fixed object like a scrummage machine can be an indispensable means of learning points 1–4 inclusive as well as how to strike. Two simple methods of emphasizing the need for a quick strike are, firstly, for the coach to say to a budding hooker, 'coming in, now', and on the word 'now' the hooker is expected

Fig. 10.1: Speed training for hooker

to kick the coach's hand which is held at ground level at the mouth of the tunnel. (See Fig. 10.1.) The other method is to drop a tennis ball or coin from the top of the scrum and ask the hooker to strike the object before it touches the ground.

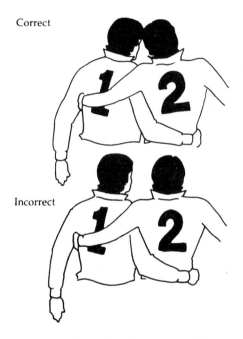

Fig. 10.2: Position of heads i.e. loose-head prop and hooker

The next progression is to bring in the props and ask them to bind. (See Fig. 10.2.) The coach should ensure that the three forwards have maximum stud contact with the ground and that there is a space between the left or loose-head prop's feet for the hooker to strike the ball. (See Figs. 10.3 and 10.4, over leaf showing the three channels of a full scrum.)

The put-in is 1 metre from the scrum and the ball must be angled so that when it touches the ground it fits the shape of the hooker's right instep, thus giving maximum control over the ball.

The hooker takes weight on his left or near foot and so is

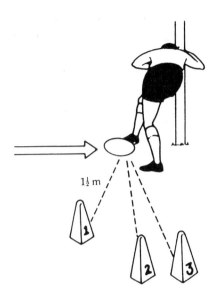

Fig. 10.3: Coaching hooker to hit channels

poised ready to strike for the ball. The scrum half now ensures that the ball goes into the scrum from midway between knee and ankle in one forward movement.

When the two locks are added (as in the Midi scrum), clearly it is necessary to introduce the concept of a second channel or exit for the ball between the left prop's legs and then between the left lock's legs. (See Fig. 10.4.)

Another simple way of ensuring that the forwards do under-

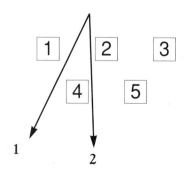

Fig. 10.4

stand precisely which is channel 1 and channel 2 is for the coach to crawl through the channels in turn – believe me, if the coach can get through, and he can, then it should be very simple for the ball. Most boys never forget after this demonstration!

The way the game has developed at senior level suggests that the skill of striking for the ball against the head is probably redundant, but some may nevertheless like to consider the following:

HOOKING AGAINST THE HEAD

The next stage is to check on how competent your team are at striking against the head; that is, when the opposition scrum half is putting in the ball.

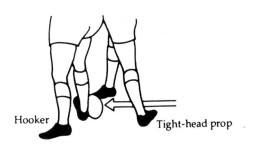

Fig. 10.5: Hooking against the head

The tecnique of your hooker is to stop the ball with his are virtually impossible to use in a Mini or Midi game, the coach sweep it back with his far foot. The really observant person will have noticed that the prop's left toe is turned out so as to bring the hip into close contact with that of the hooker; and it's this contact that helps to make for a very tight bind.

COMMUNICATION BETWEEN BACKS AND FORWARDS

It is important that the forwards know *before* they go into the scrummage which direction the ball is going. It's an important piece of knowledge because it means that the forwards ought to get to the breakdown quickly. This communication is achieved by signals from the fly half to the scrum half and then to the forwards. For example, if the fly half taps his right leg it means – YES, the backs are going right. If he taps his left leg it means – NO, we are going left.

Before the forwards go down in the scrum the scrum half must call clearly either YES or NO, before adding 'coming in now'. On the other hand, in most scrums today the scrum half must react to the hooker who taps the back of his left or loose head prop indicating he (the hooker) is ready to strike for the ball. Once the forwards are down in the scrum it is too late to signal: they can't hear. Even in Mini scrums the three forwards will have too much to think about. Although back-row moves are virtually impossible to use in a Mini or Midi game, the coach may care to know that if there was a back-row move called then all the scrum half would need to do to inform his fly half that he wasn't getting the ball was to give him a 'thumbs down' signal with either hand.

There is no doubt whatsoever that the performance of a team can be revolutionized by introducing this degree of communication between forwards and backs.

Remember . . .

The true test of a coach is whether or not the players have the confidence to try in a match what they have endeavoured to learn in practice.

Final checklist . . .
(1)   Understand the principles.
(2)   Go down as a UNIT.
(3)   Chin up.
(4)   Feet back.
(5)   Squeeze with hands.

(6)   Look left on 'ball coming in' or immediately before 'tap' by hooker.
(7)   Drop knees on 'now'.
(8)   Snap shove, that is, pull with hands/arms, straighten your legs then lock knees until the ball is out of the scrum.
(9)   Signals between forwards and backs.

10.2 THE LINE-OUT

Whether it is a Mini, Midi or a full fifteen-a-side line-out the success of the team throwing-in is governed by:

(1)   The accuracy of the thrower-in.
(2)   The skill of the jumper.
(3)   The reaction speed of other line-out forwards.
(4)   The realization that 'variation' in the numbers in the line-out and therefore where the ball is thrown, is essential.

The line-out is first introduced at under ten years of age in England with one forward throwing in and the other two in the line-out which extends from 2 to 7 metres from the touch-line. Rightly, options are very few but principles 1 to 3 above do apply and have to be taught. If you are teaching Mini or Midi Rugby you might find the following helpful in broadening your knowledge.

In the full line-out (eight forwards) there are three basic positions to which the ball is thrown:

Front: that is, to player No. 4 standing two from the front – used in defence (the front peel can also be used as an attacking ploy).

Middle: that is, to player Nos 4 or 5 – when wanting to move the ball to the backs.

End: that is, to player Nos. 6 or 8 in the line-out (assuming the hooker is throwing in), when wanting to move the ball to the backs or to execute the peel.

Fig. 10.6: The front jumper at work

Assuming the thrower-in is capable of a fair degree of accuracy, the second key factor, that is, the skill of the jumper, needs to be stressed. It is possible to display a greater variety in the timing of the jump at the front of the line-out because (a) the jumper has a better view of the ball, and (b) he is less crowded than, say, the middle jumper.

In the middle of the line-out the problem is (a) the jumper does not get such a good view of the ball (crowded), and (b) the ball has to travel further to him and therefore could be intercepted. Basically, the middle jumper aims to take the ball in front of his opponent although if he really fancies his chances he may be happy with a lobbed throw.

At the end of the line-out, unless a catch and drive is planned, the ball is either deflected straight to the scrum half from the second player from the end of the line-out (usually the No. 8) or a peeling movement in-field is attempted.

The third key factor involves the timing of the support from the players immediately in front of or behind the jumpers. Essentially, these players are trying to move in towards the jumper to give him support and protection and, at the same time, drive forward . . . or to stop opponents interfering with their jumper.

All support players should face the opposition – after all, you can only drive forward with your legs and with your body pointing towards them.

The fourth, and last, principle is the need for variety. What I mean by variety is:

(a)   Jumpers should develop different ways of taking the ball, for example, hard and low, top of their jump, lobbed, dummy forward followed by a step back, deflection, etc.

(b)   The scrum half should call for the ball (he is the eyes of the forwards) and vary the timing of the ball's delivery from the line-out so as to make the opposition uncertain – upset their rhythm.

(c)   The line-out should begin at a different time – particularly with an emphasis on getting the ball in sooner; this requires speedy communication between the thrower-in and whoever is giving the line-out calls.

(d)   As the last player of the opposition arrives the ball, on occasions, should be clearing the head of the furthest player in the line-out.

(e)   Line-out numbers should be reduced on occasions but usually only when the team throwing in is moving forward.

Remember, a two-handed catch means the line-out is not over and opposition three-quarters must keep behind their 10-metre offside line (or 7 metres for Mini and Midi Rugby).

PRACTISING THE LINE-OUT

(1)   Whilst a thrower-in must practise for accuracy against a cross-bar, goal posts, etc., the real work only begins when he is throwing to one of his jumpers. Here it is the timing or co-ordination between thrower and jumper that is crucial.

   The ball must always be thrown with the line of touch in mind. Inexperienced players make the cardinal mistake of practising with the ball being thrown at or immediately above the jumper which does not – in fact cannot – happen in a game because the law demands that the ball is thrown down the line of touch. A small but important point.

(2)   The next stage is to introduce the unopposed line-out; in other words, all the forwards and scrum half. The object is to make sure that everyone understands the signals. The rest of the backs can join in later.

(3)   Next, bring in limited opposition; either less than the full complement, or place conditions on them, for example:
   (a)   bump the jumper but do not jump against him;
   (b)   try and go through the gaps – hopefully none will exist.

(4)   Finally, practise against full opposition but moving up and down the pitch and using both touch-lines. This is to ensure that:
   (a)   the jumpers have to use not only their good hand (remember, most people are right-handed, right-footed) but;
   (b)   the captain/pack leader will get into the habit of calling the appropriate line-out according to the position on the field;
   (c)   the captain/pack leader will get used to making up his mind before the forwards arrive at the line-out (as the law demands);

(d)   a sense of urgency in the organization of the
        line-out will begin to take shape.

It is the easiest practice in the world to give one pack the prefix
A and the other B and for the coach to run to a ball(s) which
has been strategically placed on the touch-line(s) before the
practice commenced. As the players approach the appropriate
ball, the coach calls out the letter of the team that he wants
to have the throw-in. The practice now becomes realistic.

10.3 KICK-OFF AND RESTARTS

For youngsters of under eleven playing Mini Rugby, the
time is ripe to practise what at first glance may appear to be
a relatively minor skill of the game. Yet to lose all kick-offs or
restarts from the equivalent of the 22-metre line, would be to
surrender probably 10 per cent of primary possession. Experience
suggests that this is a luxury few sides can afford. If the coach
has been working on the skills of the place and drop kick, the
actual kicks won't in themselves present problems.

What the kicker will find the most difficult is to keep the
ball in the air sufficiently long for the forwards to be under it
when it alights. Actually it is a simple mathematical problem.
How quickly can the chasing forwards arrive at any given points
in the opponent's half of the field? Because that's how long the
ball has to be in the air. After all, you do not want to give the
receivers a free catch! What surprises me is how few coaches see
the importance of practising the chasing of their own kick-off or
the receiving of their opponents.

YOUR KICK-OFF e.g. Mini Rugby (nine players)

Fig. 10.7 (over leaf). How long does the ball have to be in the air for
X1, X2, X3 to reach it?
Note: you can, of course, kick it in any other direction
but your chasers need to be organized.

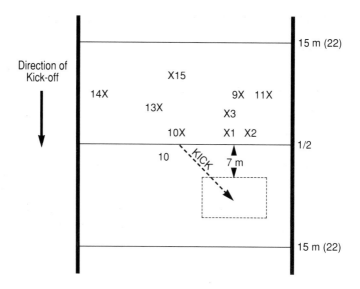

Fig. 10.7

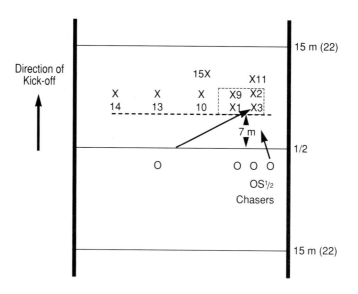

Fig. 10.8

RECEIVING KICK-OFFS e.g. Mini Rugby (nine players)

(1)   Fig. 10.8. A clear call is required.

(2)   If time permits you may have the option of attacking down the short- or blind-side.

(3)   You may have to catch and maul leaving your scrum half to use his eyes and judge what to do next.

15-METRE DROP-OUT (equivalent to 22-metre drop-out)

(1)   Fig. 10.9. The kick should be close enough and high to guarantee that X1, X2 and X3 can reach the ball at least at the same time as the opposition. There is nothing less satisfying than chasing a lost cause.

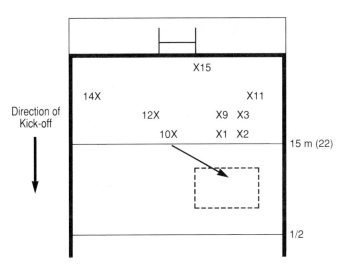

Fig. 10.9

11

TEAM ORGANIZATION

* RECIPE – BLACKCURRANT AND LEMONADE

If you've worked hard in understanding the game and the principles involved from Chapter Three then you will already have some fairly clear idea of what this heading is all about. You will understand the four principles of play and can read the 'Road Map' which is your route to success. If these concepts are still difficult to grasp then maybe a jigsaw analogy will be easier to work out – putting the various pieces together. What you now need is either further clarification or a reminder of why some teams function so smoothly and others don't.

Do the players understand what sort of rugby they are attempting to play?

Perhaps, like many players and coaches, you have not even given this a thought. Imagine, if you will, that a letter was to drop through your letterbox tomorrow morning saying, 'You have been selected to play for the Barbarians, please confirm your availability.' Having got over the initial shock, I do believe that you would be able to answer the above question because the Barbarians have developed an attitude to rugby which, in turn, has created a pattern or style of play. In essence it does not matter materially which players are selected by the Barbarians – the end result in 80 to 90 per cent of their matches is the same. The pattern or style referred to is based on players being prepared to take calculated risks and to run the ball irrespective of what part of the field they find themselves in.

If I now suggest that you have been selected for New Zealand or Australia, I suspect you would know also the type of rugby expected of you because both of these countries have created their own special identity. We in England have, through our national schools and colts teams, developed a driving forward game harnessed to no-nonsense, hard and direct running backs. This success at what may be termed youth level, has also been transferred to England teams of recent seasons, so much so that I do believe anyone selected to play for the England senior team would have a pretty clear idea of what was expected.

Now, if you were to apply the same type of thinking to the sort of rugby that is played at your school or rugby club, you should be able to answer the question. If you cannot, then I suggest you have not thought sufficiently about what you are trying to achieve, and your practical preparation for the game sounds either slipshod or non-existent.

DO YOU UNDERSTAND THE SEQUENCE OF WINNING?

A reminder of the sequence.

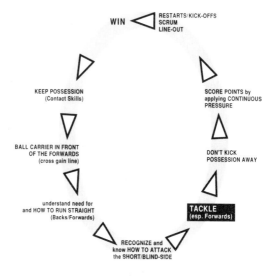

Fig. 11.1

(1)   In England, the rules for those under ten years allows them to start the game with a free pass, above that age and right up to and including the fifteen-a-side game, one team or the other kicks off from the centre of the halfway line.

Keeping possession is as vital here as it is to win your own scrums and line-outs.

(2)   Develop your contact skills, including tackling, so that the hard-won ball is never lost – this is your goal.

(3)   Assuming you have developed high levels of skill in contact then the trick is to find ways and means of

getting a ball carrier across the gain line; in other words, a ball carrier (who may be a back or forward) in front of the rest of the team. Once this is achieved your support play will automatically become easier.

(4)   Understand the need for backs and forwards to run straight; generally for the backs this means parallel to the touch-line. For forwards it may mean this as well but also remember to keep off touch-lines and make for the near goal post.

(5)   Practise, practise, practise . . . recognizing then attacking the short- or blind-side of the field. It is nearly always the least defended.

(6)   You cannot carry anyone in your team who cannot **tackle**. Look at your forwards in particular. Two of the three Mini forwards, three and a half (!) of the Midi forwards, six of the eight forwards in the fifteen-a-side game *must* be able to tackle. The days of the 'donkey' concept associated with the forwards is long since dead. Everyone has to strive to develop the mantle and demeanour of an athlete . . . in other words an athletic rugby player.

(7)   Do not kick possession away. Unless you have a kicking strategy so that everyone knows who is kicking from which part of the field, everyone is certain that the kick will go where intended and chasers have been appointed – you would be strongly advised to keep the ball in your hands. Remember even the best kick only gives you a fifty-fifty chance of regaining the ball.

(8)   Either with the ball or without it, your task is to cut down dramatically the time and space that opponents have to think and move. This we describe as keeping the opposition under continuous pressure. They begin to lose their mental resilience because you have persuaded them to believe that they are playing against twice as many opponents.

(9)   The natural outcome of executing this sequence is that your opponents will make mistakes and you will score *points*.

(10)   Any breakdown in this sequence or chain and it's back to winning primary possession – usually from the scrum.

DO YOU UNDERSTAND THE PRINCIPLES OF TEAM PLAY? I.E., GO FORWARD, SUPPORT, CONTINUITY AND PRESSURE

Now, it's no good asking a player if he understands the principles of team play because he may well be able to recite them backwards and yet not be able to demonstrate them when playing; and it's understanding and being able to apply them on the field that count. The players in a Midi scrum that goes down in ones and twos instead of as a unit of five clearly do not understand that their chances of winning the ball are drastically reduced by this action. Backs who run across the field, who shovel the ball towards their own goal line to a team-mate who is clearly in a worse position than themselves, do not understand the principles of team play. These and many more actions demonstrate clearly what the coach has or has not been doing!

DOES EACH PLAYER KNOW WHAT HIS TEAM-MATE IS TRYING TO DO?

Obviously, scrum half and hooker must be in total sympathy with each other's needs as far as putting the ball into the scrum is concerned. The hooker who strikes the ball too hard, which causes it to shoot madly out of the back of the scrum, is hardly in tune with the requirements of the scrum half. If the outside half persists in running the play down the left side of the field from most scrums, then he should be made to realize that the easy way for his scrum half to pass the ball is the direction in which the ball is put into the scrum – in other words, to the right. What the fly half has been doing is making life harder than it need be for the scrum half.

The wing who consistently overruns his centre is not only doing the side a disservice, but is almost certainly creating merry hell for the centre. There is nothing more annoying for a centre than to turn to pass to his wing only to find that the latter is in front. Equally, a wing will soon get depressed if every time the centre gives a pass it is at ankle height.

Having sympathy with, and an understanding of, the playing requirements of those immediately around you is the hallmark of a class player and something the coach must strive to achieve.

Many coaches are good at analysing the strengths and weaknesses of their own players but for some reason they never communicate their knowledge to the players.

COMMUNICATIONS BETWEEN PLAYERS, BETWEEN UNITS: DOES IT EXIST, IS IT AS GOOD AS IT SHOULD BE?

Players should talk to each other, not shout. This will ensure they all know what is happening, where it is happening, when the action is taking place and who are the principal participants. Without communication between forwards and backs you will never achieve the third principle of team play, namely continuity. Make sure the half backs have a clear system of signals between themselves, that the scrum half keeps the forwards informed, and the fly half the other backs. If the opposition are putting the ball into the scrum, then it is up to the fly half to bring the backs up to the offside line, that is the imaginary line running through the heels of the last player on their side of the scrum and parallel to the goal line. At a line-out it will be the imaginary line drawn parallel to the goal line and 7 metres from the line-out (Mini and Midi Rugby).

If by chance the fly half is going to kick diagonally for his wing on the open side of the field, then the latter should know that such a kick is expected. The old dodge of the outside half holding a hand to his ear should be sufficient for the alert, attacking wing to see and therefore to take up an appropriate position. At all costs avoid the 'I thought it was your ball' situation by careful planning and plenty of practice in the following units of the game.

KICK-OFFS, INCLUDING 15-METRE DROP-OUT (equivalent to 22-metre drop-out)

Your kick-off:

(1)   Who is taking the kick?

(2)   Forwards on one side, backs spread out on the other?

(3)   Where is the ball going to be kicked? Long, or short over the 7-metre line?

(4)   Which of your players are going to be there when the ball arrives?

(5)   Has one man been deputed to attempt to catch the ball before the opposition?

(6)   Is the field covered?

(7)   Does each player know what he is going to do if the ball comes to him?

Where the opposition are dropping out, I like to have a prop on one side of the kicker and a centre on the other. The players then have the same type of role whenever their team are receiving kick-offs. The coach, of course, may choose others to carry out this duty – so long as everyone knows what they are meant to be doing the choice is not that important.

SCRUM

(1)   Forwards must know in which direction the ball will be taken before the ball is put into the scrum. This ensures that you have the maximum number at the breakdown before the opposition.

(2)   If the opposition win the ball, the scrum half should inform his forwards when it has 'gone' and in which

direction. So, for example, he might say 'ball held', 'ball gone – left'.

(3)   Forwards and backs must know whether a back-row move is planned. In the case of the backs, as they are not now receiving the ball, they will have time to adjust their alignment.

(4)   Defence round the scrum must be organized and very much hinges round the scrum half, especially as there are no back-row players in either Mini or Midi Rugby. Remember the scrum half not putting in the ball has to stay behind the offside line running through the hindmost foot of his scrum until the ball emerges from the other team's scrum. Clearly, both scrum half and outside half must be able to tackle.

(5)   How do you defend against an extra man in the line, i.e., full back?

Does full back take full back?

Does wing step in and take full back, i.e., if the full back comes into the line outside the centre? Is it possible to drift out one place if the full back comes into the line outside the centre, i.e., centre takes full back and wing stays with wing?

What happens if the full back comes into the line between fly half and centre?

RUCKS/MAULS

(1)   In attack: do the players understand the need for leading with their shoulders, driving with their legs and grabbing shirts? Are they adaptable enough to ruck if the ball is on the ground, or maul if it is held in the hands?

(2)   In defence: does the scrum half look after the short- or blind-side of the field?

What happens if a centre is on the ground in a ruck? Who covers his position? The last forward to the breakdown?

PENALTY KICKS

(1)   Your ball: who always gets his hand on the ball?
       e.g. scrum half? Who decides whether to kick for
       touch, move the ball, kick at goal? Captain? Pack
       leader?

(2)   Their ball: how do you defend? Mark your opposite
       number?

CAPTAINCY/PACK LEADER

No coach, let alone player, knows all that there is to know
and, therefore, captain and pack leader (they may be one
in the same person) must help each other. A captain is not
simply the player who decides which end to attack – this role
is much more encompassing, and the good coach will see it as
of paramount importance to develop the art of captaincy.

After all, the coach cannot play the game. At practice
sessions, the coach should give the captain and/or pack leader
some responsibility commensurate with their age, ability and
experience. He should encourage the captain not to abuse
players publicly but to speak to them quietly and firmly and,
above all else, to congratulate them on the things they do well.
The coach will be rewarded one hundred-fold if he broadens the
playing knowledge of the captain and tries to show him what
options are available from different parts of the field and different
situations – whether to run the ball from a penalty or to kick for
position; whether to attack down the short-side or the open-side;
whether to introduce back-row moves; whether to kick off long
or short, open or blind; these sorts of decisions can often mean
the difference between winning and losing. Captaincy is about
leadership; about whether or not you can get the very best out
of the other players. It is also about making decisions, and the
worst decision a captain can ever make is not to make one at
all.

Off the field the captain and/or pack leader represent the
link between management, including coach, and the team.
If players in any team are not happy it is one of the roles

of the captain to inform management so that the issue(s) is solved before it becomes a debilitating sore. The public-speaking qualities of a captain are not onerous but they must be able to greet and thank match officials and opponents in a friendly and civilized manner.

Add all these factors together, answer all these questions, and you should have a well-adjusted and successful team who enjoy every minute of each other's company.

DO YOU UNDERSTAND WHAT YOU ARE SEEING?
GAME DIAGNOSIS – THE DUTY OF EVERY COACH

First of all it is necessary to understand what is meant by the term diagnosis.

If ANALYSIS means breaking down into constituent parts, for example, the number of scrums in a Mini Rugby match, who won them, etc., then DIAGNOSIS equals ANALYSIS plus the correct treatment to effect a cure.

The attributes of a coach should include his ability to diagnose a game effectively. By this, I mean he should be able on the one hand to see what is going right or wrong, and on the other, be able to remedy any faults. Plenty of people are capable of deciding what is going wrong, but few would know how to remedy the fault. With Mini Rugby players, correcting faults is so important. The fly half who is dropping the ball on almost every occasion will be abundantly obvious to one and all, but what will be less obvious is why he is dropping the ball and especially what steps should be taken to eliminate this sort of error. It is the difference between observing secondary effects and primary causes.

There is a great temptation to view a rugby match purely as a cinema show, with images flashing by, and your eyes following the ball everywhere. Everything can be marvellously exciting and whilst obviously you must do this on occasions, there is also much to be learned from watching players who have not got the ball, players who are perhaps picking themselves up from a scrum, and players who are walking.

At the end of the match, not only should you have a

mental picture of how the game flowed, whether your side was principally attacking or defending, but you should also know why you lost the scrums or rucks/mauls and what action you will take at your next practice session.

Probably the best position of all would be to have a helicopter-view of the game, but as this is quite impracticable, you must do the next best thing – alternately view the game from the side and end of the pitch. Where Mini Rugby is being played there is no problem in changing your viewing position and so, at the end of the match, you should be able to build up a very accurate picture of what happened, and why it happened.

Points you might look for when viewing from the side:

(1)   Gain and tackle lines: do the team understand their importance? In other words, do they understand the need to go forward?

(2)   Alignment of backs: steep or shallow? Do they move together? Do they dog-leg in defence?

(3)   Kicking – effective or ineffective? Kick-offs too long? Touches missed?

(4)   Overall continuity of the game – is it good or bad? Are players aware of the need to keep the ball available on contact and if necessary to switch the direction of the play?

(5)   Is quality possession being obtained from:
        (a)   Scrum-snap shove? Locks packing down at the same time as the three front-row players? (Midi Rugby.)
        (b)   Ruck – forwards fast enough to breakdown point? Never go in empty handed.
        (c)   Maul – ball being screened and secured? Players staying on their feet? Does the scrum half call for the ball when he wants it?

(6)   Support in the scrum, ruck and maul. Does everyone seem to know his job? In attack as well as defence?

Shoulder contact in support? Forwards supporting on each other's hips? Where do attacks start? Own half? Opposition's? Counter-attack?

(7)   Is the line-out organized quickly and preferably as the team throwing it in are moving forward? Is it clear that everyone knows the signals? Is the thrower-in accurate – does he give the jumper/catcher a reasonable chance to use his skill? Does the supporting line-out forward(s) know his job or does he stand looking totally bemused? It is obvious that the thrower-in has another role once the ball has left his hands . . . or does he look totally bemused?

Points to look for when viewing end on:

(1)   Handling: are the backs 'taking the ball early'?

(2)   Straight running:
         (a)   Backs – to cross gain line? Coming up on the inside of their opposite numbers?
         (b)   Outside half has his chest facing you? or shoulder?
         (c)   Forwards – into rucks, parallel to the touchline? In general play do they keep movements going straight?

(3)   Variations:
         (a)   Backs – alignment and approach of players taking the ball in a switch.
         (b)   Forwards – screening the ball, shoulder going in?
         (c)   Support – positional play in attack and defence. Do forwards know their duties?
         (d)   Forwards – where do they cover? Scrum channels?
         (e)   Scrum half 1 metre from scrum?

These are some of the tell-tale signs indicating that the coach, and therefore the players, understand the game.
    Even to observe or collect any of this information a pen-

cil/notebook, tape-recorder or, nowadays, a video camera will not go amiss, because it is remarkably difficult to remember small, but probably important, items a few days later when you are preparing the school or club Mini Rugby practice session.

Incidentally if you are one of those enthusiastic fathers with trembling hands, don't show the whole of your video 'master' in one sitting. The excitement generated will be overwhelming and learning nil. However, it's your skill as an editor of video that will make all the difference. Generally, a piece of video of no longer than 3 to 4 minutes' duration is quite sufficient for the very young. Not only does their retention skill not last long but, like us all, they need to be trained to sort the wheat from the chaff. They, like you, should be looking for primary causes and not secondary effects.

Only by skilful question and answer will you and they grow to realize the real value of video and place a proper perspective on what they think they are seeing.

12

CHOOSING YOUR PLAYING POSITION

The overall heading and aim of the section is well meant. *All skills to all players* has to be the long-term aim. During the Mini and Midi learning stages young players will hopefully experience a number of playing positions, not only depending on their physical characteristics but on their mental inclination. For example, if a player does not like the repetitive close-quarter bodily contact associated with forward play then no matter if that player is 6 foot 6 inches tall and built like a gorilla, or a scaled-down mini version, he will not conquer what his brain is telling him.

The following guide-lines will hopefully give a flavour of each position and help the young player to choose wisely.

12.1 FORWARDS

GENERAL POINTS

(1)   Winning possession of the ball in scrummages, line-outs and kick-offs is the priority of the forwards; for this reason it is often said that forwards win matches – you can have the fastest three-quarters in the world but without the ball they might as well go home.

(2)   As a forward you must be relentless in your pursuit of the ball; your aim is to win good ball and win it going forward; to achieve this aim and give continuity to the play you should always be up in support as soon as possible and you should be able to use many of the skills normally associated with the three-quarters; there are very few moments when you are not actively involved.

(3)   You have to be athletically mobile.

(4)   Winning has to start in the front row because unless you are prepared to impose your will on your opponents, then rarely will your team be in a position to 'go forward' and that is the prerequisite of a winning side.

(5)   Young players should learn first of all how to handle their own body weight through such exercises as:

press-ups, dips and rope-climbing, etc. Forget weight training until the late teens and only then if you are being instructed by a qualified person on how to lift safely and the type of lift and weight suitable for your level of maturity.

PLAY – PROP

(1)   The basic role of each prop in the front row of a scrummage is to provide strong support for the hooker, to enable the latter to concentrate on making a clean strike for the ball.

(2)   The loose-head or left prop, the player who wears number 1 on his back, has perhaps the more difficult role to perform; as a loose-head, your responsibility is to ensure that your hooker can see the ball, and to do this requires a combination of strength and technique to keep your side of the scrum high enough.

(3)   When the front row goes down it is the tight-head prop on the right-hand side of the scrum who makes contact first.

(4)   The front rows crouch, eye-up their opposite numbers, pause and the tight-head takes the initiative by stepping forward with his right foot and making contact; from then on you can adjust the position of your feet either to push the opposition on their ball or prevent them from pushing you on your ball.

(5)   You must not only go down as a unit but you must be tight with each other, that means your binding must be firm and secure.

(6)   It's the loose-head who binds on to the hooker first on your own put-in, followed by the tight-head, but remember, it is the tight-head who engages his opposite number first.

(7)   The skill of a prop forward at a line-out is either to

Fig. 12.1

support one of his jumpers by stopping opponents from impeding his jump or to move quickly to where the ball is being thrown. Frequently the prop at the front of the line-out moves in-field, either to collect the ball or to help initiate a drive.

(8)   As the prop in the middle of the line-out you have to be able to support either the jumper in front of you or the one behind.

(9)   The prop makes a point of placing his feet as close to the line of touch as the law will allow, because he knows his opposite number will be just as keen on coming forward and taking his space; if you stand 6 inches too far away you will give your opposite number an unnecessary advantage.

(10)   When the ball is thrown to the back of the line-out there is a greater chance of losing possession because the co-ordination required between the thrower-in and the catcher has to be so precise; as a supporting forward you must be always on the alert in the expectation that the ball will be deflected.

(11)   When receiving a kick-off you'll face the standard question, do the props stand in front of the locks or do they stand behind? The answer is very much up to the

individual players, the important thing is that the ball is secured, which means the props must move quickly to their own catcher.

(12) If a team can win set ball, that is from scrum, line-out and kick-off, then it is in a position to begin to dictate play. The next thing is to attempt to disorganize the opposition defence and create space for attack. As a prop, once the ball is in open play, your contribution will be dependent entirely upon your skills of running, handling and tackling.

(13) Handling skills will be required most often in tight situations under pressure from the opposition. Close handling by the props needs practice; you have to work as a unit, so you must know how to present the ball to each other. Through repeated drill you will discover your individual strengths and build up the instinctive reactions you need in a match.

(14) As a prop, you are generally last to arrive at the first breakdown and therefore have to act like a flanker; this means that you have to make crucial decisions. Do you pick up the ball and drive forward? If the scrum half is trapped, do you take his role? Should you bind on to the left or right side of a ruck or maul? Can you see the ball?

(15) To do all of this a prop forward must know where the breakdown is going to be – helped by signals from your scrum half, you need the mobility to get there and, once you arrive, the ability to make correct decisions.

(16) Speed off the mark is just as important for a prop as for any other player and it's important that you learn how to run correctly; this skill in itself will increase your ability to run fast.

(17) As a prop you will be selected primarily for your scrummaging ability and your support play in the line-out; however, if you have any ambition then you will have to make a major impact on all aspects of loose play.

PLAY – HOOKER

(1)   The less spectacular but more conventional skill for a hooker is to win your own scrum ball with a quick, clean strike.

(2)   The other common role of the hooker is that of the thrower-in at the line-out, which also requires considerable skill, but your role at the line-out doesn't end with the throw; you must follow the ball, keeping up the pressure, and help to regain possession; it's an enormous bonus if, as a hooker (No. 2), you can bring running, handling and contact skills into your game; these will allow you to be as effective as any back-row forward in loose play.

(3)   Supporting on the side of a maul or driving into a ruck, these are the decisions of loose play that you have to make as each situation develops, decisions based on your understanding of the game and your anticipation of what is going to happen next. They may be simple actions in themselves but they can have a major effect on the success of your team.

(4)   As a hooker your body must be flexible, particularly in the hips and shoulder girdle when striking for the ball. You need acceleration from a standing start over 20 to 40 metres and the ability to repeat this type of running many times over in a match. If you want the speed of a flanker as well as the contact skills then clearly your training must reflect these demands.

(5)   Another feature of training should be contact work to develop a combination of a bodily toughness and the techniques necessary for meeting contact situations on your terms.

(6)   At the line-out, as a hooker, your throw must be consistently accurate so that the jumpers can depend on receiving good ball.

(7)   Try using the goal post as a target for the throw. Orange markers are spaced out 1 metre apart starting 5 metres from the goal post and extending to the 15-metre mark. Throwing from this near position is equivalent to throwing to the front of a line-out; moving back along the line of markers increases the distance, representing throws to the middle and end of a line-out.

(8)   What this practice doesn't do is to take into account how the jumper would like the ball to be thrown; timing is the key and this can only be developed through practice with the jumpers themselves. Clearly on the long throw both timing and accuracy become even more critical.

(9)   If, at the line-out, the ball is passed to the three-quarters, you should just follow the ball as quickly as possible to the next breakdown.

(10)   In part, the hooker's role at the front of the line-out is similar to, and just as important as, the flanker's at the end of the line-out. The hooker has to be the master of the 5-metre area or any other area which represents the short- or blind-side of the field; you should be prepared to sweep up untidy ball and, in general, to protect the scrum half.

(11)   When you are close to your own line everything becomes much more critical; the accuracy of your throw and your defensive role thereafter.

(12)   As a hooker you will feel that you have greater freedom of action when you're in your opponent's half; mentally you're under much less pressure, defence is less of a priority, you should be prepared to take a chance; however, no matter where you are on the field if you are alert you will be able to capitalize on your opponent's mistakes, the hallmark of all top-class players.

(13)   As a hooker you should remember to lead with your right shoulder as you go down in the scrum, having bound firmly over the shoulders and under the armpits

of the props. The tight-head prop (and the right flanker – fifteen-aside game only) and the right lock should be exerting sufficient pressure on you to the left so as to keep you as close as possible to the put-in.

(14)   No scrum can hope to function successfully unless the scrum half and the hooker are on the same wavelength. A hooker must be sharp and accurate in his striking. It's vital for the scrum half to feed the scrum so that the ball lands at such an angle that it fits the shape of your boot.

(15)   The hooker does not decide which channel to strike down, he is waiting to hear from the scrum half whether or not a back-row move has been called; if it has then the ball will tend to be struck to channel 2.

(16)   There's nothing dull about playing hooker; to play with a number 2 on your back requires many skills; you have to have an excellent throwing arm, the strength of a prop forward coupled with the agility of a gymnast, good hands and the speed and tenacity of a flanker to chase kicks until you drop. It's a guarantee that you will be always in the game.

PLAY – LOCK

(1)   The constant, relentless pursuit of the ball by the locks – Nos. 4 and 5 – calls for many qualities, not least of which are durability, strength, stamina and speed.

(2)   A powerful jump is essential but power alone is not enough, individual technique and co-ordination with the thrower-in are also vital; at the front of the line-out speed of thought and action is the key.

(3)   As a lock forward you should never jump at the same time as your opposite number, you must either jump before him or after him; if you can develop more than one type of jump you will always keep the opposition

SETTING UP AND
WINNING THE BALL
IN RUCKS AND
MAULS

THE POWERHOUSE
OF THE SCRUM

Fig. 12.2

guessing. With the lob ball you take a dummy step forward to fool the opposition and then take the ball jumping backwards on to the support of your prop. This demands perfect co-ordination with the thrower-in which will become possible only after considerable practice.

(4)   The front of the line-out can also be used as an attacking ploy especially if you are close to an opponent's line.

(5)   Although good handling skills with a ball in the air are basic and vital to your role in the line-out, under the pressure of a match it isn't always easy to make the perfect catch with two hands.

(6)   In general, as a lock forward at the front of the line-out, once the ball has gone over your head you should follow the ball.

(7)   Three-quarters will tell you that they want early ball without the attention of opposing back-row forwards because it gives them time to make decisions: ball

from the middle or end of the line-out achieves both objectives because the opposition back-row forwards are engaged in either jumping for the ball or in supporting those who are.

(8)   You must have line-out signals so that you know where the ball is going – firstly, if it's your ball, it is then up to you to make sure that the thrower-in knows precisely what type of jump you are about to employ; secondly, remember you'll never win the ball by going straight up and down, you must go forward, you must cross the line of touch. The line-out is not a vertical exercise but a horizontal one – think about it!

(9)   The middle of the line-out is a very crowded area and the true skill of the jumper is being able to win possession and then deliver the ball quickly and safely either to another forward who is looking for deflections or directly to the scrum half.

(10)   In a scrum the two locks must act like Siamese twins; you are there to provide the power base to enable the front row to do their job properly and win their own ball.

(11)   Your binding must be tight: you pull your second-row partner towards you with your inside arm bound either just below the armpit or on the far side of the waistband and, at the same time, you each pull your respective props on to you with your outside arms bound either round the hips of the props or between their legs; if you elect to bind between the legs it is normal to grip the prop's waistband or wrap your arm round his inside leg. As the scrum goes down both locks, in unison with the rest of the pack, should drop their knees and drive forward as the ball comes in.

(12)   The right lock can play an important part in either stopping a wheel or slowing it down, provided, of course, he's got the necessary strength.

(13)   It's generally accepted that the left-hand lock has a harder job to do on his own put-in than the right-hand lock; he has to give the loose-head prop the best chance of keeping the scrum high enough so that the hooker can see and therefore strike for the ball. This means tucking your left shoulder under the buttock of the loose-head prop and remaining rock steady. If your loose-head prop and hooker are under pressure from the opposition tight-head prop this is no easy task.

(14)   Having strong arms is one of the essential ingredients in the tackle, tenacity is another and the grappling and wrestling qualities needed in the close combat of forward play.

(15)   Few sides seem to realize the importance of kick-offs and 22-metre drop-outs. As the number of restarts has increased so has the burden on the locks who are expected to have the bravery and skill needed to secure possession.

(16)   As the receiving team, the most difficult kicks to deal with are the ones where the ball hangs in the air and gives the chasing forwards a good chance of arriving as the ball lands.

(17)   At a drop-out, the most difficult kicks are those aimed about 5 metres beyond the 22-metre line because, again, you know the opposition can reach you. In each case you must catch the ball, turn, and bring it down quickly, trusting that you're being protected by your other forwards.

(18)   The direction in which you must run from scrum ball will become intuitive with experience. On your own scrum ball your scrum half will put the ball in on the left-hand side and, if it's won, then the play will tend to drift to your right. If the opposition put the ball in, on your right-hand side, then the play will tend to drift to your left. Certainly on your own ball you should have

been given a directional signal by your scrum half before the scrum has even gone down. You'll know when the scrum is over if your scrum half makes an appropriate call or you can tell by feeling when the pressure has eased from the opposition as they move the ball away – the important thing then is to get moving as soon as possible to support the play, ready to help your team to gain or maintain possession of the ball, you can't win without the ball.

(19)   At each breakdown you have to make an instant judgement as to the appropriate action required, you won't always be right but at least be positive.

(20)   The ability to become an effective driving forward is dependent upon attitude, you simply have to enjoy physical contact; it is dependent also on technique, you must lean forward so that you make contact with your shoulders which also will help to keep the ball well away from the opposition. You must pump hard with your legs, they are your driving force. No opponent is going to keel over obligingly. The locks should get used to arriving together and put their heads between and their shoulders under the buttocks of those in front of them; if you are in an upright position you can generate very little force.

(21)   Very few scrum halves initiate a system of communication with their forwards at breakdown. However, by using the code words 'up, up, up' for the ball that is going to his own forwards, the scrum half can help you (the locks) and front-row forwards to be up in support of the ball.

PLAY – FLANKER

(1)   Whether you play open- or blind-side flanker, whether you're big or small, you must have speed, and your first target is nearly always the outside half.

TARGETS FOR THE
OPENSIDE FLANKER

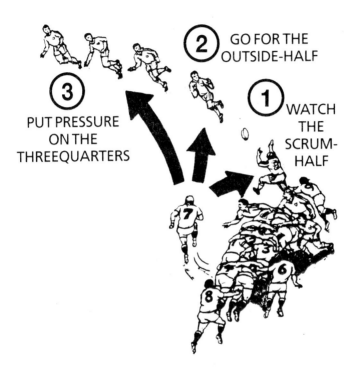

Fig. 12.3

(2)   The flanker's first task at a scrum is to push, because
       if he doesn't and the scrum goes backwards, then the
       opposition outside half will have a definite advantage.

(3)   At the line-out, your role as an open-side flanker
       is either to protect your own ball or to get into a
       position to pressurize your opponents – be aware of the
       opposition scrum half in case he attempts to break.

(4)   Winning the ball in the air is not considered to be
       a primary skill, but it does have obvious advantages.

(5)   At a line-out stand *in-field* of your opposite number,
       keep yourself free to put pressure on the outside half.

(6)   As the open-side flanker keep yourself *in-field* of the line-out maul allowing yourself an unimpeded run at the opposition three-quarters.

(7)   Always assume that something might go wrong and stay on the alert all the time.

(8)   If your three-quarters are given the ball your principal objective is to support the ball carrier, but, in so doing, a skilful open-side flanker will actually take the same running line as his opponent, making it very difficult for the latter to get at your three-quarters.

(9)   On your throw-in begin by standing level with your opposite number – this gives you the opportunity to move either in front of him or behind him – after all, you know where the ball is being thrown and he doesn't. However, at the precise moment that the ball is leaving the line-out on its way to your fly half you should aim to be running from a position in-field of your opposite number. The one who masters this crucial positional skill is the one more likely to dominate the running lines at the back of the line-out.

(10)   The ability not to get trapped into a line-out maul is the hallmark of an experienced open-side flanker – remember aim to be on the *in-field* side.

(11)   The blind-side flanker's job is to stop the first player coming round his side of the scrum (could be the scrum half or the No. 8).

(12)   The blind-side flanker must position his head in the scrum so that he can see the ball, which will allow him to judge the best time to disengage from the scrum.

(13)   The blind-side flanker, normally standing three from the end of the line-out, has a variety of roles. In general, once the ball goes beyond him, his job is to follow the ball and support the play.

TACKLING THE
BLIND SIDE
ATTACKER

HEAD TO THE SIDE

ARMS GRIP
TIGHT

DRIVE OFF THE
GROUND

Fig. 12.4

(14) If, as a blind-side flanker, you can develop some line-out ability, you will give your team another line-out option.

(15) Continuity of play can be achieved only if you have reliable handling and contact skills. Picking up the ball and instantly getting to your feet is a skill which has to be mastered if you are going to keep the game flowing. An intuitive knowledge of how your fellow back-row forwards will react to any given breakdown situation can only be developed by playing and practising with them regularly.

(16) No opponent is going to hand over the ball willingly, he's going to hang on to it until he feels he's got some

support from his own team. Upper-body strength and endurance are essential to all players especially the flankers because one of you should be first to most breakdowns; if it's you then it's your job to win, or help secure, possession of the ball.

(17)   There needs to be a close relationship between the No. 8 and the two flankers because they perform such a vital role in maintaining the continuity of play. It is essential all three have a hunger to arrive as one at any contact situation. The first player will make the ball available, the second player will keep the continuity going and the third player will be a further link man if needed. You need the hands of a juggler combined with the strength of a wrestler and the power of a charging rhino!

PLAY – No. 8
YOUR ROLE AT THE SCRUM

(1)   If your forwards are dominating the scrum then the best time to pick up the ball is as the scrum snaps forward. However, even if the scrum is not going forward, provided your hooker has struck the ball cleanly to your feet, if you pick up immediately you'll still catch their back-row forwards and the scrum half off balance.

(2)   While the right-hand side of the field is the best side for a back-row attack, at the same time the defence are alert to this possibility. It's helpful, therefore, if your fly half can make a great show of creating a diversion in the opposite direction.

(3)   You must have good communications, either verbal or through a system of visual signals; sometimes a designated side of the field will have a code word, for example, 'yes' equals right, 'no' equals left; as a back-row forward, you need to know whether the ball is going close to the scrum or out to the midfield and whether the kick is going to be high and hanging, deep

or short. All these factors will influence your chosen running lines.

(4)   As the hindmost player in the scrum, the No. 8 is in an excellent position to take a last look at the opposition and make a mental note of what they are likely to do should they win the ball. Each of your flankers should know that it is their responsibility to take the first opponent who comes round their side of the scrum – your job is to take the second opponent irrespective of whether he comes left or right.

YOUR ROLE AT THE LINE-OUT

(1)   By tradition, the No. 8 is the third line-out forward after the two locks, and normally stands either two or three from the end of the line. In some teams he might stand right at the end or even act as a principal jumper at the front or middle of the line-out if his talents are in that direction; having established your value to the team you take up your position accordingly.

(2)   It's important for a No. 8 to be able to react quickly to the ball that has been deflected from another player especially if the ball is likely to hit the ground towards the end of the line-out – this is potentially dangerous.

(3)   Although not all line-out balls are taken cleanly in the air, it is where initial contact with the ball is made and so the No. 8 and locks, as the principal catchers in any team, must spend time working with their hands above their heads.

(4)   Once you're out of your 22, for some line-out players an accurately deflected ball may be the only means of winning reasonably quick ball for the three-quarters. Normally, to attempt a deflection in your own 22-metre area is potentially dangerous because if it doesn't go into the hands of your scrum half, the opposition back row will be on to it . . . and that spells trouble.

(5)   As part of the back-row trio you should be on the ball throughout the game, supporting one another, competing to get to the ball first and always staying on your feet – what you are trying to do is to maintain the continuity of play.

(6)   In these actions it is important to adopt a low driving position as you approach a loose ball. An upright body position presents a much easier target for the opposition to stop than a low driving one. You must develop the attitude of driving forward with your body angled to the ground, it's the only way to capitalize on your handling skills and strength.

REMINDERS FOR ALL FORWARDS

(1)   For the prop: you are the pillar of the scrum and a support player in the line-out and the loose.

(2)   For the hooker: you must win your own ball and, if you're the thrower-in you should be the model of accuracy.

(3)   For the locks: you're the powerhouse of the scrum and the principal source of line-out possession.

(4)   For the flankers: you should never be more than a metre away from the ball because your role is to keep that ball moving forward for your team.

(5)   For the No. 8: you must be decisive, especially at the base of the scrum; the three-quarters want quick ball.

Remember, forwards win matches, if you cannot secure the initial possession of the ball from scrums, line-outs and kick-offs then the whole team has an impossible task.

12.2 BACKS

PLAY – SCRUM HALF

(1)   A scrum half should be able to pass quickly and accurately off either hand, but you have to do much more besides.

(2)   You should always be on the move, always in support of the ball carrier, looking for opportunities to exploit weaknesses in the defence. You are the link between backs and forwards – yours is a key position for keeping the game alive.

The Dive Pass

Tactical kicking

X NO

✓ YES

NO – CUT OUT THE BACKSWING   YES – TOUCH AND AWAY

Fig. 12.5

(3)   If you can make a break you will always present prob-
       lems. Opposition back-row forwards will become wary
       of you.

(4)   A scrum half has to make a lot of decisions and the
       only way you can make correct decisions is by being
       totally aware of what is happening around you. You
       must lift your head and use your eyes.

(5)   It is essential to be in communication all the time with
       your forwards and your backs, either through words or
       visual signals.

(6)   Every breakdown in play is an opportunity for com-
       munication and good communication starts with the
       introduction of directional signals. For example, in a
       scrum in the middle of the field, directional signals
       become of crucial importance otherwise the forwards
       will not know in which direction to support the backs.
       If the scrum is close to the touch-line it's fairly obvious
       that the ball can only go in the opposite direction.

(7)   As the scrum moves away from the touch-line, space is
       created down the blind-side so that there is the option
       of moving the ball to the right or left.

(8)   You can use any system of signals or calls as long
       as everyone understands them. There are occasions
       in every game when the scrum half chooses not to
       give the ball to his fly half. For example, if there is
       a back-row move. However, the scrum half must have
       a signal to tell his fly half that he is not receiving
       the ball.

(9)   At a line-out it is easier for the scrum half to commu-
       nicate with the forwards because they are now standing
       up. The hooker needs to know where the ball is to be
       thrown, a decision quite often taken by the scrum half.

(10)   As a general rule, sides tend to use the front and
       middle of the line-out in their own half and the middle
       and end of the line-out in their opponents' half.

A long ball has the advantage of tying up the opposition back-row forwards but demands a much more accurate throw from the hooker.

(11)   The timing of the pass to the backs should be varied so that the opposition cannot predict your every move, but bear in mind that backs prefer to receive the ball early rather than late.

(12)   Don't assume that you can't have signals with your forwards at rucks and mauls, because you can. For example, if you call 'up, up, up', this can mean that the ball is going to the backs, if you call 'down, down, down', it means you are going to link up with your forwards. These call words are intended purely as examples, use whatever you prefer. The principle remains the same.

(13)   There are many refinements you can make to your system of calls. For example, you could add a directional signal to the call 'down, down, down' so that the forwards know whether you are breaking to the right or left.

(14)   With experience you begin to anticipate what is about to happen next, so that you are no longer relying entirely on signals, you are in fact using your experience and your ability to anticipate. The link with your forwards and the probing of the opposition defence are complementary skills which you must develop.

(15)   As scrum half you always have to be in the correct position to pass. From a line-out, this is a position closer to the touch-line than the catcher of the ball. In this way you do not have to turn your back to the line-out, you are moving into the ball, you can see their back row and you can therefore judge right up to the last moment whether to pass or do something else. This means you must learn how to pass off either hand.

(16)   Passing is not just a hand action, it is a whole body movement. When you practise you should always have a target, preferably the fly half, the man you're going to partner in a match. Speed of pass is much more important than length, and to achieve this you have to eliminate back swing. You want the ball in your hands for as short a time as possible, whether it is coming out of the air or off the ground.

(17)   You bend your knees, place your hands on the ball and in one movement sweep each ball in the direction of your fly half. *Note*, as you place your hands on the ball virtually all your weight is on your rear foot, your other foot acting as an arrow, pointing in the direction of where you are going to pass the ball. It is a continuous and rhythmic action; first watch the ball in order to put your body in the correct position and then concentrate on the target.

(18)   As a scrum half, it's particularly important that your trunk, shoulder, arm and neck muscles are strengthened because it is this upper area of your body which comes into regular physical contact with your opponents.

PLAY – FLY HALF

(1)   The most important job of a fly half is to get his three-quarters on the move, to get the ball down the line, hopefully to the wing as quickly as possible, to make it a nine-man or a fifteen-man game and get the whole side running forward.

(2)   There are two ways of getting the ball into the winger's hands. The conventional method is to pass the ball to the centres and then on to the open-side wing which often makes an exciting spectacle. However, the more hands the ball goes through the more chance there is of error, which is why many fly halves opt to use the blind-side wing on the short-side of the field – the

quickest and safest way of bringing a winger into the game.

(3)   As a fly half each situation has to be judged on its merits. The quality of the possession received from the forwards is the most important thing. Occasionally, quality of the pass from the scrum half will dictate that you can't pass the ball on, but on the whole it is the overall quality of the ball given by the forwards.

(4)   Few forwards seem to realize that the backs want *quick ball* whether it is from scrum, ruck, maul or line-out, but even when quick ball is given you may opt to kick if it suits the tactics of your team.

(5)   Even if you choose to kick you have first of all to catch the ball . . . which means you must have safe hands. You should have your own rugby ball to practise activities like throwing and catching, picking up the rolling ball, and as many other activities as you can think of, so that the ball becomes a natural extension of your hands.

(6)   Develop the link between yourself and your scrum half; vary the length of the pass between yourself and your scrum half by calling for a short or long ball.

(7)   Successful communication on the field depends upon verbal and visual signals but it also depends upon a deep understanding of the game and each other's role.

(8)   The link with your centres is very important as the rest of the three-quarter line must appreciate what the scrum half and you are trying to do. They must know all the signals and they must know when the ball is coming out from the forwards and what moves are being called.

(9)   Although as a fly half your prime function is to get your three-quarters moving, it is extremely helpful if you have the ability to make a break or a half-break because it takes the pressure off your three-quarters by disrupting the defence.

(10)   When considering if a break is possible you should
        observe the alignment that the opposition are using
        against you. The only realistic situation where a break
        is likely is if the defence are not coming up in a line of
        three and leave a little gap. Perhaps the inside centre
        has come up too quickly in front of his fly half, leaving
        a little gap for you to go through . . . assuming you are
        astute enough to see their mistake.

(11)   From line-outs you have a little bit more time and if
        you can beat the open-side flanker you can make a full
        break, or a half-break and 'pop' your centre through
        the gap.

(12)   What is the defensive role of the fly half? From scrum
        half ball you should go up on to your opposite number
        bringing with you your two centres who should take their
        own man.

(13)   A drift defence is used by some teams from the line-out.
        It means that if you are fly half and defending from a
        line-out, you automatically drift on to the opposition
        inside centre. You all move along one player. The
        opposition fly half is left to your open-side flanker.
        It means that you all 'drift' across the field and try
        to push the opposition sideways into touch.

(14)   If you see an opposition full back or winger coming
        into the line it all depends on the type of defence that
        you are using. If you are using a man-to-man defence
        then it is very simple. It means that you are more or
        less defending in channels, so if somebody comes into
        your channel you must take him.
            If you are drifting in defence and an extra man
        comes in, you must spot him early. If he is coming in
        between their fly half and inside centre then you, as fly
        half, must take him. If the extra man comes in outside
        their outside centre then your outside centre drifts into
        him. Try and persuade your open-side wing to keep out
        and look after his opposite number.

(15)   As an outside half you need a variety of kicking skills.

If you are kicking from outside the 22-metre line remember that you have to develop the ability to bounce or roll the ball into touch.

Like it or not, and most spectators don't, accurate kicking is the easiest way of getting into your opponent's half of the field. Although kicking means you loose possession, if everyone knows when and where you are going to kick, and the chasers are organized, you will get the ball back.

(16)   The purpose of practice is to develop a sound technique which will never let you down, no matter how much pressure you're under. Never practise aimlessly; you should always give yourself a target. (Use cones.)

Place kick

Touch kick

Fig. 12.6

(17)   The perfect kick from inside the 22-metre area should bounce no more than 1 metre over the touch-line, this ensures that none of your power is wasted and the ball travels the maximum distance.

PLAY – CENTRE

(1)   Whatever their size, centres have to be powerful players, always in the right position and they must have reliable hands. As a centre space is always limited because opponents are constantly on top of you. You must not waste possession and never stop running to support the ball carrier.

(2)   The most important requirement of a centre is an ability to make openings for his winger. To do this you obviously have to be able to catch and pass off either hand and time the pass correctly. A lot of centres just pass the ball automatically but it is the timing of the pass which is important. This means the most opportune time for the receiver, not the passer. It's a split-second judgement.

(3)   As the passer of the ball, you should move towards the defending player before releasing the ball. Straight running is very important because you can't depend on your fly half keeping a line totally straight.

(4)   An inside centre has to tackle head-on occasionally if, for example, opponents attempt the switch but, on the whole, it is easier to tackle by using your speed and letting the man go for the outside and then taking him from the side.

(5)   If the defence is marking man-to-man from scrummage ball, then it is important to throw in a mis-move to reach the wings quickly or to introduce an extra player in order to sow seeds of doubt in the opposition defence.

(6)   Centres take their defensive lead from their fly half, if he is out of position their job is made doubly difficult. Defence is all about good communications, about who is marking whom. You have to talk an awful lot to your fly half about moves, about defence. The fly half may call a drift defence especially if he knows he can get from his man to the inside centre. Be ready.

(7)   It is very difficult to say when it is possible to make a break in the centre. It may be that the defence has drifted too early; then your best option is to keep the ball.

(8)   A break can occur if the opposition outside centre makes the simple mistake of getting in front of his own inside centre. This gap can be exploited by your inside centre.

(9)   Even from scrum ball where the opposition are so close to you, there are spaces to be found for you to put your wing in the clear, but to do this you must have:
          safe hands;
          quick hands;
          the ability to move the ball on instantly;
          the ability to give a properly timed pass;
          the knowledge and the ability to straighten the line;
          physical presence in the tackle, and in contact situations where it is essential that you retain possession of the ball;
          the courage to take on opponents bigger than yourself.

(10)   Straight running is not easy but it is vital. There is a tendency for fly halves to run a few paces sideways before passing the ball but, as a centre, you can compensate for this.
          Note how many paces your fly half runs with the ball before passing it to you. Add the number of paces he takes to your normal starting position – you will now be able to pick a straight running line.

The technique is to run slightly back towards the player who is about to pass.

(11)   A centre must be able to ruck and maul. He is often the nearest player to the man who is tackled and therefore should go in to try and secure the ball before opponents arrive.

(12)   To get ball from line-outs and scrummages the defences are very organized and they can stifle you. From rucks and mauls they are not as organized, giving those vital few seconds longer in which to make decisions and to use your skill.

(13)   Prepare yourself realistically for a very demanding position. Most of your work will be repetitive, requiring short bursts of activity placing high demands on your energy reserves. Shuttle running should form a part of your training programme.

Speed off the mark in the centre is a great asset.

(14)   As a centre you will play many matches without there ever being the opportunity of making a break and yet play an incredibly important role in helping those around you to be part of a winning team.

PLAY – WING

(1)   You have got to be looking for work, it's pointless just sitting on the wing expecting things to happen, you have got to make them happen.

(2)   Your speed is fundamental to your game. Speed and the ability to beat the opposition are qualities that all top-class wings must have.

(3)   When the wing gets the ball, the tempo of the match should immediately increase, you have been selected for your speed, so use it.

(4)   You need the speed of a sprinter over 30 to 60 metres

but the difference is that you will probably have to repeat it several times in a match.

(5)   Natural ability will take you so far, but only the discipline of regular and correct training will take you to the top.

Fig. 12.7

(6)   If you train all year round you will develop a high plateau of fitness from which it is much easier to reach your peak.

Note: there is much evidence in an increasingly car-dominated life-style, that young people do not naturally exercise in a manner that is appropriate to even a healthy life-style, let alone in a manner appropriate to preparing them for rugby.

Parents would do well to use the car sparingly and encourage their children to walk, jog or cycle wherever possible.

(7)   You have to work in close harmony with your full back and centre. For example, the switch pass is particularly useful if you find yourself running out of space or if you spot that by coming inside, you will wrong-foot the covering defence.

(8)   The skill of beating an opponent needs to be worked on. But you must first of all convince the defender that you are going to break on his inside, before you attempt to go round him. If you have speed and acceleration it is generally better to beat an opponent on the outside.

(9)   As a defending wing the basic rule is that you should move towards your opponent to cut down his thinking time.

(10)   Although the side-step tends to be a slower action than the outside swerve, it can check opponents before the change of direction is effected.

(11)   Wings must also develop defensive skills; you are expected to be rock steady under high kicks. Remember, if the opposition think you will panic under the high ball, it's a safe bet that they will kick even more in your direction.

(12)   Generally speaking, the left wing has to do more defending than the right for two reasons: partly because play has a natural tendency to move in this direction, and partly because most scrum halves and outside halves

are right-footed and find it easier to kick tactically in the direction of the defending left wing.

(13)   If a back-row or a three-quarter attack takes place within the 22-metre area in the direction of the defending left wing, then the attackers tend to have the advantage. Again, don't wait for them to come to you – move forward to tackle.

(14)   It's extremely helpful to have wings who can clear their lines in defence with either foot. One-footed players can be a liability in many tight situations.

(15)   There's no secret about tackling, everyone should know how to do it, the skill is in reading the game well enough to anticipate where you will be needed.

(16)   In tackling it is normal to force the ball carrier to your outside so that he has only one direction in which to run. You must then drive in hard and low and hang on until he's firmly grounded.

(17)   A wing who is prepared to run from deep position, in other words to start a counter-attack, will always cause his opponents to panic. Give it a go.

(18)   Perhaps the ultimate quality of a wing is always to be in support and able to react in a spontaneous way.

PLAY – FULL BACK

(1)   If you want to get your name on any team sheet as a full back, your defensive qualities must inspire confidence. Safety under a high ball is of paramount importance, it demands courage and good technique, don't let the ball drop.

(2)   If you are safe and sure in defence, you will inspire confidence in your team – this is your first priority.

(3)   If you have pace and a willingness to attack, you will also be in great demand.

(4)   Ideally you should be able to kick with either foot.

(5)   If you gather the ball outside your 22, because the law does not allow you to kick the ball directly into touch, you must develop the skill of bouncing the ball in the field of play before it crosses the touch-line; this requires considerable practice to perfect. The technique involves kicking the ball hard into the ground, 2 or 3 metres in front of you, so that it bounces end over end into touch.

(6)   It's not always possible, or tactically desirable, to kick for touch but if you choose instead to kick ahead, you must always follow up quickly, to keep the opposition under pressure.

(7)   In general, from a scrum, you stand some 10 to 15 metres behind your three-quarters on a line roughly between your centres. Always keep your eye on the opposition scrum half in case he does not pass but chooses to run.

(8)   The secret of tackling is being in the correct position and this is only possible if you know the type of defence that your three-quarter line is operating. It is vital that you talk to each other so that you all know who is marking whom.

(9)   As the last line of defence you have to be unbeatable in the tackle. No matter how you bring the man down, bring him down you must. The problem is how to get close enough to make effective contact.

       The answer lies in anticipating the running lines of the ball carrier, by aiming low and driving through him and just hanging on until you bring him to the ground.

       As you become more experienced your timing will improve and you will make fewer mistakes. But it is always a contest, the advantage of which tends to lie with the ball carrier.

(10) The bonus for a full back comes if you have a sense of timing and sufficient speed to join your three-quarters in attack. But you have to ask yourself if you are coming into the line to punch a hole or merely to act as an extra pair of hands. In the former case, you will come with much greater speed and power than the latter.

(11) The insertion of a full back down the short- or blind-side can easily create an overlap.

(12) In counter-attack you must have confidence and a high level of intuition between yourself and your wings which will only come through practice and match experience.

   By its very nature, a counter-attack will always have the element of surprise.

(13) Remember, your first priority is to gain the confidence of your team as their last line of defence. You must always be in the correct position, anything else is a bonus.

REMINDERS FOR ALL BACKS

(1) For the scrum half: you must be able to pass.

(2) For the fly half: you need to know how to get your three-quarters on the move.

(3) For the centre: you should have the ability to make openings for your wing.

(4) For the wing: you must have speed.

And behind these four positions . . .

(5) As full back you should be able to read the game with certainty so that you are always in the correct position.

THE SUPPORTING CAST

13

REFEREEING MINI/MIDI RUGBY

'You can play a match without a coach but NOT without a referee.'

This rather sobering statement may, at first glance, seem a nasty smack in the eye for Mini/Midi Rugby coaches but that would be to ignore reality; and reality is that most coaches of Mini/Midi Rugby are also, by accident or design, referees. In spite of what the pundits might say, 99 per cent of players couldn't even tell you who had refereed their game, let alone any of the finer points of the art of refereeing. Again, this is not an admonishment of players, rather a compliment to the referees, for generally it is only the bad referee that is remembered.

If you detect strong personal views in these remarks then you are absolutely correct, for my experiences over the last twenty years have brought me into contact with referees at all levels – from the pedestrian performer with the 5ths to the razor-sharp at international level. I have also had the good fortune to listen to a wide range of very talented referees expounding on their art from the doyen of them all, Alan Bean, who refereed from the 1940s to 50s, before becoming a teacher of referees, right up to Fred Howard and Ed Morrison (England) and Jim Fleming (Scotland), Stephen Hilditch (Ireland) and Derek Bevan (Wales), the top names of the 1990s.

Not surprisingly, when you have digested all that these referees have had to say, certain common threads emerge which apply at whatever level you are refereeing. As each player is different in physique, ability, etc., then so too is every referee and each will contribute to the game his own personality and method.

The next time you watch a game ask yourself the following questions:

(1)   Did the referee's performance contribute to the enjoyment of the game?   **Yes/No**

(2)   Did he establish a good rapport with the players? **Yes/No**

(3)   Was the referee physically fit enough for the game? **Yes/No**

(4)   Was he generally in the right positions to make the important decisions?   **Yes/No**

To me, if any referee or adjudicator can honestly answer 'yes' to these questions, then the referee is doing a worthwhile job.

The referee is judge and jury of both fact and law on the field. Whether they like it or not, players and spectators must recognize this, but what shows through and picks out the top referee is his personality, how he goes about his task, and whether or not he is able to promote enjoyment. If he has any other motivation he is probably in the wrong recreation.

When very young boys of, say, under nine or under ten are playing Mini Rugby the mistakes are often many and a problem arises – 'What do I let go?' Most experts will tell you that the spirit and flow of any game lies in the observance of the laws. All I can advise is to be consistent and to be positive. Remind Mini Rugby players in all practice sessions of what the laws allow them to do.

Give them advice but if they wantonly disregard it then they should be penalized. Personally, I believe *offside* is so detrimental to the development of an orderly pattern to the game that the Mini Rugby referee should not hesitate to warn, for example, anyone who is in even a marginally offside position, yet not interfering with the play, to desist from this practice forthwith and then to penalize him if he persists. Remember, all offside offences are penalized by a penalty kick. If you have penalized the scrum half for not standing 1 metre from the scrum as he is putting in the ball, make certain that your metre does not become ½ metre or 1½ metres as the game wears on.

Consistency is essential. Do not work on the tit-for-tat basis; in other words, if you make a mistake against one team do not feel that you have to make it up by awarding them a penalty or granting them a dubious try.

Occasionally, even Mini Rugby players innovate, and yet how many referees blow their whistle the moment something happens that they do not recognize. If the referee were to ask himself the question, 'Why shouldn't I allow it to happen?'

this will at least give an opportunity for the advantage law to apply. A referee who runs round the field with the whistle permanently to his lips clearly has the wrong approach. On the other hand, when a referee does blow his whistle the sound should make quite plain whether he is blowing for a penalty (a firm blast) or foot up in the scrum (free kick). A good referee is quite capable of making his whistle 'talk'! He should also use, if he so desires, the signals approved by the International Rugby Football Board.

The Mini Rugby referee starts with some extraordinary advantages over the man taking a fifteen-a-side game in that, by virtue of height, he can see right over the scrum, line-outs, rucks and mauls and, in four or five strides, can cover an area of the pitch that may take ten or twenty mini-strides by the young players. This, of course, can lead to many bad habits, like cutting corners or even remaining stationary – habits which would prove fatal for the maintenance of firm control in the senior game.

If you really want to learn more about positional play then watch a good referee but, above all else, get yourself along to your nearest referee society – you will be pleasantly surprised how helpful the Hon. Secretary can be. I would merely illustrate the art of refereeing by asking you to note the position of the international referee when there is a scrum or line-out near the goal line. You can bet your life that he will have read what is on and be waiting in the in-goal area for the player to ground the ball for a try. No players, and this includes Mini Rugby players, are going to think much of you if one side is claiming a try and you are chugging some 15 or 20 metres behind.

The other area of refereeing which is very important is advice offered to young inexperienced referees. They are always told not to watch the ball that is kicked high into the air. They can rest assured that the ball will come down and by raising their eyes skywards they may miss a blatant offside or late tackle.

All referees must have a degree of fitness commensurate with their ambitions and, at worst, the level of game they are refereeing. Make certain before you referee that you have a pencil, score card, coin, whistle, watch and a ball! It is not a bad idea to check the perimeters of the ground so that you know how long the in-goal area is. If the game is being played across a full pitch and someone thought they had the bright idea of using a goal line as a touch-line with two hard senior goal posts in the path of the unsuspecting winger, then don't referee until the touch-line has been moved at least 5 metres from the goal line.

Check that the goal posts are padded and that there are no foreign objects like iron girders or concrete posts so close to the touch-line that they might constitute a danger. Don't discover at half-time that no-one is running the line. If youngsters are acting as touch-judges make sure before you start the match that they know their duties. This sort of preparation can help make for a smooth-running and enjoyable game.

Now, it is no accident that I have quite deliberately left the peculiarities of the laws of the game to last, because I do believe you can make an excellent job of refereeing without being able to quote chapter and verse of the laws. However, there are certain facts about the laws which you must understand and that begins with the definitions. Certain words are used in a way of which the dictionary might not approve. For example, in a rugby context 'in front of' means 'with both feet', except when unsuited to the context. The word 'dead' does not mean someone has expired but that 'the ball for the time being is out of play'. Laws have to be read most carefully and not in isolation, for it is no good considering Law 24 Offside without reading the scrummage, line-out, ruck and maul laws, as they are all interconnected.

Apart from reading and studying the laws and the accompanying notes, you need both to visualize practical situations on the field and to link in the minds of the Mini Rugby players the laws with the practical word you are giving them.

For as much as, and for as long as, I've heard referees being told that they should never go to bed without the laws of the game beside them (a strange bedroom activity!), I would remind referees and coaches of Mini Rugby that the laws are not merely words on a piece of paper, but the practical parameters and the spirit of a marvellously dynamic game of physical contact which has been shaped by trial and error for over one hundred years. There is no point in blaming the laws for your shortcomings for the good as well as the bad games have been played under exactly the same conditions.

WHERE DO I STAND? WHICH WAY DO I MOVE?

In fact, it's advisable to keep shifting your position particularly at line-outs, rucks and mauls because you would be amazed at how many crafty players there are who will be up to no good if they suspect you are rooted to the same spot.

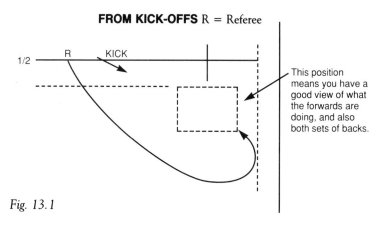

Fig. 13.1

This position means you have a good view of what the forwards are doing, and also both sets of backs.

FROM LINE-OUTS

Ask yourself who is throwing in. Am I close to the goal line? If the answer is yes, I am close to the goal line – that's the direction you move. You must be in a position to determine a try.

In any event don't stay at the front – move, probably towards the non-throwing-in team. But always glance over your

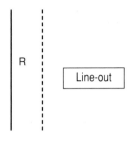

Fig. 13.2

shoulder to check that the non-throwing-in backs are behind their offside line. Look out for hookers who stroll round the front of the line and obstruct the opposition scrum half even without touching him! Watch for the open-side flanker at the end of the line-out – he will try and start chasing their fly half from an offside position by standing beyond the length of the line-out. Don't think it was an accident!

FROM SCRUMS

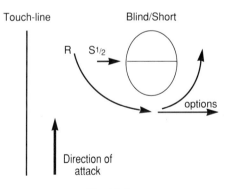

Fig. 13.3

Start behind the scrum half who is putting in the ball and slightly to his side of the scrum.

Check that the scrum half is 1 metre away and the ball does go into the scrum straight. After it has been hooked, start thinking of moving to follow the play as indicated.

FROM RUCKS/MAULS

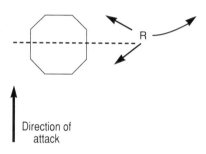

Direction of
attack

Fig. 13.4

Don't stand still. Watch for who went in with the ball, the fringers, particularly the non-ball carriers. Look over your shoulder for the defensive three-quarters – keep them behind the offside line. That is the imaginary line running through the hindmost foot of the last player in their scrum.

FROM HIGH KICKS

Don't watch the ball. It will come down! Watch the kicker, and anyone on his side who is in front of him – be suspicious. Watch defenders who place a screen of players in front of their receiver – it's called obstruction and you should penalize them.

14

RESPONSIBILITIES

14.1   CLUB

The last ten years have seen some surprising, and at times confusing, changes in patterns of who plays the game and the environment in which they have been taught.

Basically, there are more schools affiliated to the England Rugby Football Schools Union (approximately 2,900) than ever before, certainly since the inception of the parent union, the Rugby Football Union, in 1871. Yet there is a marked decline in the number of schools in the State system who are regularly turning out 1st XVs. Historically, from team games being extremely popular and a part of the ethos of the school, much has changed. Many other sports, both team and individual, have emerged over the last fifty years. So much so that every governing body of sports has been pursuing with vigour the attention of youngsters in an attempt to persuade them that their activity is the best.

In the 1980s we were faced with a period when competition was denounced by a number of so-called progressive experts in the field of physical education; they said competition was unhealthy. They conveniently forget that life was itself a competition for jobs, etc. Fortunately, most of those thinkers are now out to pasture. An air of realism has returned.

School teachers then had a period of dispute with their employers and one consequence was that after-school activities almost ceased. Happily this situation is now being reversed by many teachers . . . but not all. The Government, through the National Curriculum Council has launched a new appraisal system for pupils which, like any change, is being resisted by some, and even for those who are enthusiastic, the workload for teachers appears to have increased considerably. Rugby, it seems, may be on the school timetable but only as one of a number of 'invasion' games. Soccer, hockey and lacrosse are examples of games where one team invades the space of the other, hence the term 'invasion' games. It's unlikely that any more than two hours per week for six to eight weeks will be spent on all invasion games, which of course means that rugby may or may not be taught depending entirely on the interest and enthusiasm of individual teachers.

Most Rugby Unions have not been sitting on their bottoms or twiddling their thumbs during this period. The Rugby Football Union, in recognizing that these changes were in the pipeline, have ensured that each county in England has at least one Youth Development Officer whose job it is to promote rugby in the schools and clubs. Perhaps the most innovative feature has been the promotion of a non-contact rugby game called New Image particularly designed for the junior schools where classes are mixed and the majority of teachers are women. Again, the last ten to twenty years has seen a positive move to have mixed PE classes in Junior Schools and therefore to devise a game where boys and girls could play in harmony was a prudent move.

The RFU was also responsible, through the good offices of Tony Butlin at the University of Sunderland, for devising separate cross-curriculum packs for junior and secondary schools. This meant rugby could be taught through every subject of the curriculum. Well over 5000 junior schools took up the free offer. This response reflects a market that had remained untapped for over one hundred years and probably owes a lot to the marvellous performance and positive publicity associated with England reaching the final of the 1991 World Cup, winning back-to-back Grand Slams and World Sevens Champions in 1993.

At this point one also has to pay tribute to the enthusiasm of rugby clubs who, in response to the many changes in State education, have opened their doors to youngsters on a scale quite unprecedented. However, before any club goes rushing headlong into Mini/Midi Rugby and all its ramifications, I do hope they have either carried out a detailed survey of the state of rugby in their local schools or are about to do so. Just as there is little point in trying to coach senior players who do not really want to make a regular commitment to their club, so there is little point in setting up a Mini/Midi Rugby organization if the local schools are already giving all the youngsters in your area an opportunity of playing the game. Let's make it abundantly clear, if local school teachers are taking the trouble to introduce and develop rugby in the schools, leave well alone.

One of the organizational problems/challenges which has

evolved since Mini Rugby was introduced in 1971, is the sheer number of youngsters who have been recruited. This has presented clubs with an administrative and coaching manpower problem that, in some clubs, still causes great difficulties.

In a number of clubs, the Mini Rugby section is larger than the senior club membership and the comment, 'What is it, a Mini Rugby club or a fifteen-a-side rugby club?' has been heard frequently. Not unnaturally, many senior members feel they are being swamped by screaming kids and, what is worse, they cannot get near to the bar! One of the simplest solutions to this state of affairs was arrived at quickly by some bright sparks who immediately organized a soft-drinks-only bar at the opposite end of the club house to the main bar. This helped diffuse the situation but, of course, it did not solve it.

It is vital that all volunteers see it as a part of their responsibility to the youngsters in their charge that they at least attend an RFU Start Rugby Course and then become qualified Preliminary Award Holders.

Whilst in the short term clubs have to rely on volunteers, it is a mistake to settle for volunteers indefinitely, particularly on the coaching side.

The possibilities of using rugby as a means of educating youngsters in desirable social habits should not be overlooked. One of the important principles of the game is, as we have seen, 'support'. In other words, on the field you rally round to help a colleague who is in difficulty; the same principle should apply off the field in club activities and, of course, in life in general.

Those clubs who miss this golden opportunity to educate in the widest sense might just as well ask themselves why are they involved in a team game like rugby football. Why not ten-pin bowling, squash or all-in wrestling?

Some schools really do help to educate their pupils using a variety of methods and experiences. They, in fact, act in *loco parentis* whilst the child is in their care. I would suggest that this is a role which clubs will increasingly have to adopt as well as abiding by the principles of the Children Act 1989.

Without delving into the many facets of this complicated problem, it is fair to say that the old days of rugby without any compunction is rapidly giving way to an almost complete freedom of choice.

In this situation, if a boy or girl then elects to join a rugby club you can be reasonably certain that they have done so either of their own free will, or because of the desire of their parents. The onus is on the club not to disappoint the young player or parents, and this means good organization based on a sound club playing policy.

The aim should be to have a playing or coaching committee which decides the policy and seeks the right people to manage and coach the respective teams or squads of players. It is essential that those involved in Mini Rugby do like children. This is a point I have made before and it is so blindingly obvious that it should not require being said.

Many Mini Rugby people tell me that finance is not a problem, in fact the increase to club coffers through bar profits and social functions has been most encouraging, but what has proved a problem is that changing and bathing have been under immense pressure. Initially, some facilities were Calcutta-like until either extensions to existing facilities could be made or a rota system was introduced. In some instances, the number of young players involved has considerably increased the wear and tear on the ground(s) itself, and this is a problem less easily conquered. Leaving aside what might be termed club and player responsibilities, I believe there is much merit in looking at the subject of communications, not only those which affect club members (and here I would include a school rugby club in the same context), but the relationship between a club and the general public.

So often the club notice-board is the only means whereby the members are informed of what events are taking place. Therefore, to see yellow-stained notices is somewhat depressing especially to the casual visitor.

A notice-board needs to be large enough to be seen and continuously up-dated with correct information presented in a lively manner. A club newsletter can also help to create an identity and, at the same time, inform a wide audience of what is happening. It's not a bad idea to send the newsletter to the local newspaper, referee society, St John Ambulance, and to guest speakers that have helped you out or whose services you would like to call upon at some time in the future.

A few clubs have really revolutionized their communications with considerable benefit all round. No rugby club is an island, but a part of the local community.

There is a very apt line in the 'good book' which implies that by giving you receive, and this came home to me quite forcibly in New Zealand two years ago when delegates at a congress related how their senior club members had all trooped down to the local hospital twice each season to give a pint of blood. Whilst Mini Rugby players cannot do this they can certainly help the 'old folk' on an organized basis and also those children less fortunate than themselves (e.g. handicapped), by sponsored runs. I do believe this is an area of communication as yet largely untapped and one which would help to promote an awareness in the eyes of the community that rugby clubs and players do care about others.

If you are trying to recruit players then contact the head teachers of local schools to see if they will allow you to advertise on their school notice-boards, and do not be afraid to advertise what you can offer in the local newspaper or via the local radio station. Car stickers are another popular means of advertising, as are T-shirts, ties, blazers, etc. There is much to be said for creating a club identity – be proud to be seen!

The following may prove of help to those clubs involved with young players. They could be described as prudent.

PLAYING SURFACE(S)

(1)   Good playing surface clear of stones and potholes.

(2)   A clean pitch, avoiding the use of inorganic fertilizer and creosote mixtures to mark out the pitch, particularly those containing paraquat.

(3)   Padded goal posts and any barriers, projections close to the pitch.

Illus. 52: Showing flexible corner posts used at Twickenham.

(4)   Flexible corner flags which do not splinter on contact.

PLAYING FACILITIES AND EQUIPMENT

(1)   Good supply of correct sized balls, i.e., at least one per
        four players. Under eleven = size 3, under fourteen =
        size 4. James Gilbert of Rugby produce all sizes, shapes
        (and even make a large presentation ball) and colours to
        suit your taste. The balls can be for training or practice,
        matches or autographs or commemorative purposes.

(2)   Either permanent grids marked out or sufficient cones or
        plastic lids, for example fifteen cones/lids = eight grids.
        That is, four players to a grid = thirty-two players.

(3)   Scrum machine, tackle bags and tackle shields.

(4)   Lecture/projection facility, that is, a room which can be blacked out, blackboard or whiteboard, pens, chalk, duster, power points, perhaps extension cable, TV and video, etc.

(5)   Access to indoor facilities like gym or sports hall (very necessary in mid winter).

FIRST-AID FACILITIES

It was the Australian poet Adam Lindsay Gordon who said:

> No game was ever yet worth a rap
> For a rational man to play
> Into which no accident, no mishap
> Could possibly find its way

All parents, be they coaches or interested on-lookers, should be made aware of these four lines. I would suggest that accidents are a part of life and no matter how brilliant your preparation and planning, no matter how safety-conscious you are, you certainly cannot play any game, let alone a contact or collision game like rugby, without receiving an injury at some time during your involvement. It may be someone pulling a muscle with no-one within a million miles, to a broken bone as a result of a tackle or an awkward fall. However, what you do have every reason to be concerned about is if any injury is caused as a result of foul play. The laws are the framework designed to ensure a fair contest. The referee is present in his capacity as an arbiter of those laws but players need to be reminded of their responsibility to each other. As I said in Chapter Two everyone has to go back to school or work on Monday morning.

Having stated the parameters, it would not be unreasonable to expect the following first-aid facilities at a well-run rugby club:

(1)   Your club address and telephone number should be
        displayed prominently.
            It is quite staggering how often valuable time is
        lost because the caller cannot identify where he/she
        is calling from.

(2)   Every club should have a stretcher and twelve trian-
        gular bandages easily available. The stretcher should
        be in sound, working order, which means it must be
        checked periodically. You should also have a neck col-
        lar, a properly stocked medical cupboard and case which
        are kept under continuous review by the club doctor or
        physiotherapist.

(3)   At least one member of the club should attend a
        St John Ambulance Brigade first-aid course.

(4)   Someone should be on hand at every coaching ses-
        sion or match who can administer the mouth-to-mouth
        technique of resuscitation.
            Ideally, every club would have a registered doctor
        or physiotherapist in attendance but this is not always
        practical. In any event I do not see it necessarily as the
        coach's responsibility – if the senior players can admin-
        ister the resuscitation technique that would be helpful.
        In any case I believe the coach has enough on his plate
        carrying out his duties as a coach – perhaps others from
        the club should take on this responsibility.
            The Royal Life Saving Society can be very helpful
        in this respect by providing a person to come along to
        the club and give members the necessary instruction.
        Contact – The Royal Life Saving Society, Desborough
        House, 14 Devonshire Street, London W1N 2AT.

(5)   With the increase in transmittable diseases, communal
        baths are not recommended. Showers are preferable. In
        any event, where a skin infection is established, the
        player should see a doctor forthwith for proper treatment
        and not play again until free from infection.

(6)   Encourage your players to wear a mouthguard in practice
        sessions and matches.

MANAGEMENT OF INJURIES

(1)   If there is momentary unconsciousness, confusion,
        memory loss or unsteadiness, then there is evidence
        of definite concussion injuries. The player in question
        should be taken from the field and if there is no doctor
        present to offer an opinion, then take the player to the
        local hospital.

        In any event, irrespective of his age the player
        now has a compulsory twenty-one days off all rugby.
        No contact practice, no club training game, and do
        not allow the player to return to the game until given
        medical clearance.

(2)   Where spinal injuries are suspected DO NOT MOVE
        THE PLAYER – await expert attention and keep the
        player absolutely still.

INSURANCE

All clubs and schools affiliated to the Rugby Football Union in
England have a variety of complimentary insurance cover. For
further details contact The Secretary, Rugby Football Union,
Twickenham, TW1 1DZ. In any event you are advised to look
at your own personal accident insurance cover to see whether it
is necessary to top-up that automatically provided in England.

14.2   PLAYER (S)

There is a tendency nowadays for young people not to look
after their kit as well as they might – they work on the premise
that there will always be more where that came from. Parents,
in particular, are strongly urged to read this section or better

still ask their offspring to do so. It's by no means an exhaustive list of responsibilities.

(1)   Ensure that your kit is washed at least weekly and that it is named.

(2)   Have a preventative course of tetanus injections.

(3)   Where possible have available multi-studded moulded rubber-soled rugby or soccer boots for hard grounds – these will eliminate the risks of cuts.

(4)   Have boots which fit firmly over the ankle bones and are padded. The studs should conform with British Standard BS6366 1983.

(5)   Do not chew gum when training or playing.

(6)   The three front-row forwards are recommended to wear shin guards made of plasterzote (very light).

(7)   Purchase a mouthguard. Remember, you can repair a broken limb but you cannot replace a natural tooth.
       A mouthguard must be custom-made for each individual by sending an impression of the upper jaw recorded by a dental surgeon or on an upper plaster model produced by a dental surgeon and sent to a laboratory, or by using an impression kit supplied by firms like Sportsafety Limited, 23 Weardale Avenue, Forest Hall, Newcastle upon Tyne, NE12 0HX.
       The price of £18.00 includes impression kit, completed guard and strong container for keeping the guard.
       When supplying your own model or impression the price is £15.00 for a clear mouthguard and £19.50 for a coloured mouthguard of your choice.
       The completed guard is usually returned within four days of receipt of impression or model.

(8)   Ask your parents if they have, among their normal household insurance, remembered to cover you for personal accident and the loss of your playing equipment.

(9)   Control your temper.

(10)   Never argue with the referee.

(11)   Do not take unfair advantage of any player.

Remember you are playing for fun and to make friends.

14.3 TEAM MANAGER

No rugby club could function without volunteers. However, any volunteer will not do. That person must have a very keen sense of responsibility, be well organized and ensure that the player and his parents have the utmost confidence in his ability and integrity.

The following are but a few of the tasks that a team manager may care to consider. The list is by no means exhaustive.

(1)   Collect players' subscriptions and pay to treasurer. (See Enrolment Form.)

(2)   Keep a register of names/addresses/telephone numbers (up to date) and of attendance at all practice sessions. Ring those who miss – report to coach.

(3)   Keep supply of team sheets.

(4)   Collect valuables before practice sessions and each game.

(5)   Make sure all players are neatly attired with clean boots, jersey, socks and shorts.

(6)   Rugby balls to be sole responsibility of manager: ensure that ball(s) available for all practices, matches. Check correct size/pressure and be responsible for the safety of the ball(s) after each session/game.

(7)   Supply half-time orange or drink.

(8)   Supply full-time warm tea (particularly important with youngsters).

(9)   If club gear provided – be responsible for collection after match, and laundry.

(10)   Check eligibility to play for team, for example, player within prescribed age limit.

(11)   Ensure emergency playing kit available in event of someone not turning up with kit, or ripped shorts. Also have spare laces, garters, hammer and pliers.

(12)   Ensure new members, who often arrive with mum, are met and shown to the changing-room; perhaps given own peg.

(13)   Showering should be supervised for safety.

(14)   Organize transport to matches or co-ordinate with whoever does.

(15)   First-aid kit always available at every practice and match and to be sole responsibility of manager.

(16)   Look after injured players. Report injuries to club doctor without delay.

(17)   Organize visitors to hospitalized injured players.

(18)   Make sure players are informed of all club functions, social and otherwise, team or club.

(19)   Attend coaching and other meetings where coach unable to attend.

(20)   Arrange team photograph – keep photographic records.

(21)   Check availability of all managers/coaches/players three to four weeks before end of season for next season.

(22)   Maintain contact at least twice during off-season with previous season's players with view to keeping fit.

(23)   If using society referees ensure they are met when they arrive at the club and are looked after. Offer travelling expenses – saves embarrassment.

(24)   Use game to educate players – the game demands good support on the field. Ensure good support, respect for each other off-field.

(25)   If playing away from home, remember to thank tea ladies, etc. Maybe small souvenir from your club – ashtray, pennant, etc.

(26)   On away trips tip the bus driver if he's done a good job.

You may depute certain players to carry out some of these tasks but they are still your responsibility.

Example of an ENROLMENT FORM, (*Separate form for each child required*)

I would like my son/daughter to join the Mini Rugby sessions held at .... R.U.F.C.

I understand that .... R.U.F.C., its servants, agents or employees are not under any liability whatsoever for loss of property, accidents or injuries, of or to my son/daughter however caused during the course of training preparation or matches played at .... R.U.F.C. or other grounds.

*I am interested in becoming a non-playing/playing member of the club and would like to be sent an application form.

*I require .... (number of extra application forms).
(*Delete if not required)
Subscription .... per season minimum.

A card will be issued to each boy/girl on receipt of his/her subscription. (Please hand in this form, as soon as possible.)

Details (please complete in BLOCK CAPITALS)

Full Name of Child ....

Parent's Name ....

Address ....

....

Telephone No. ....

Signature of Parent or Guardian ....

SPECIAL NOTES

(1)   In England, the RFU are not keen on festivals and
       fixtures which are played on a knock-out basis with
       outright winners.
           The preferred approach is for everyone to play each
       other so that winning does not become the sole object
       of the exercise. To this end one or two thoughtful
       organizers have presented all participants with a cer-
       tificate signed by a well-known rugby personality, or
       presented every participant with a small pennant to
       commemorate the occasion.
           No-one should feel that they have failed as a Mini
       or Midi Rugby player. The object is to further their
       interest and not to kill it.

(2)   Putting on a demonstration: it has become fairly com-
       mon-place for New Image, Mini/Midi Rugby to be used
       as a curtain raiser to a big match, primarily with the
       object of promoting the idea in the minds of parents
       and youngsters that rugby is a very enjoyable game to
       play and watch. However, the end result has often had
       exactly the opposite effect because the Mini Rugby game
       simply fell flat. It was a scrambling affair with pile-up
       following pile-up and everyone either bored to tears or

feeling acutely embarrassed. This situation could almost certainly have been avoided by more careful thought and preparation. First of all, you do not pick two clubs who are deadly rivals – this is a guarantee of disaster from kick-off. I make no secret of the fact that when we put on demonstration games at Twickenham we either use teams from the same school or we have one rehearsal between different schools in which certain conditions are imposed. For example, if one team attacks through their wings then the other cannot; if one side use 'miss-out' moves then the other would probably work on the 'switch'.

On top of that the games are always refereed by a person who is familiar to the players so that he or she (yes, women have refereed at Twickenham) can talk to them during the game and actively encourage them to try things, to express themselves. This sort of sympathetic refereeing allows the game to flow which, after all, is what you are trying to show the watching and perhaps uncommitted. Remember this is a demonstration game as opposed to a normal competitive match.

Apart from playing a game, I would hope that Mini Rugby coaches would also want to demonstrate the skills of the game, especially by showing the use of grids and channels.

As you can imagine, for sixty-four youngsters to work in sixteen grids at the north end of Twickenham is some ordeal and yet, with one rehearsal, it is quite possible to show some progressive practices without the players getting in each other's way. In this sort of demonstration what looks particularly impressive is when the sixty-four boys run out on to a pitch totally free from grid-markings, carrying with them only twenty-five plastic orange cones/lids and sixteen balls. In a twinkling these cones are perfectly placed to make sixteen grids and, lo and behold, there is instant action. What you cannot see from the stands are the small pieces of paper which have been placed where the cones are to be set, nor are you to know that a rehearsal of this manoeuvre had taken place during the previous week.

With the Twickenham timetable before any big match being timed literally to the minute, this sort of planning is essential.

Give it some thought before you try your next New Image Mini/Midi Rugby demonstration game.

APPENDIX

VARIATIONS ON A THEME

Right at the outset I indicated that there was a world-wide movement away from very young players being introduced to a contact game in the learning phase and/or a universal move away from introducing newcomers to the full fifteen-a-side game.

The rugby field is simply too crowded, hence small-sided games, often with little or a total absence of contact, have been devised. Here are a few examples of what is happening in England, Wales, Ireland, Australia and New Zealand.

ENGLAND

Rugby at club level should be introduced in a gradual way from under seven up to under twelve by what has commonly been referred to as the 'Continuum'. Whilst causing all sorts of anti feeling from coaches at club level initially, and thoroughly welcomed by the teaching profession, coaches of young players have gradually come to see that the following progressive method, far from discouraging youngsters, has actually kept more of them in the game and keen to learn new skills at the beginning of each season.

THE CONTINUUM
NON-CONTACT MINI RUGBY UNDER SEVEN

Key Stage 1

(7.1)   The object of the game is to score a try (5 points) by placing the ball with downward pressure on or behind the opponent's goal line.

(7.2)   The game is played between teams of not more than five players.

(7.3)   The game is started or restarted with a free pass from the centre of the field. The starter's team must be behind the ball (i.e., nearer their own try line than the starter). The opposing team must be 7 metres away nearer its own goal line.

Note: at a free pass the ball is held in two hands and is passed to a team member. The ball must be passed through the air and not taken from the hands of the first player. At every free pass restart (throughout all the games until U11) the passer must not run with the ball and he must not dummy pass. Normal play resumes as the pass is made.

(7.4)   Initially players may pass the ball in any direction. When the players are comfortable with the ball, sideways and backward passing can be taught.

(7.5)   If a player running with the ball is touched with two hands below the waist by an opponent, the player must pass the ball as soon as possible and certainly within three strides. Opponents must not prevent the passer from passing the ball.

Note: the three-stride rule is not intended to allow a player to continue to score a try, but if a player in the act of scoring a try is legally touched a try shall be awarded.

Note: it is helpful for the referee to indicate that a 'Tackle' has been made, i.e., that the player has been touched, by shouting 'Tackled'.

(7.6)   If a player – legally touched – fails to pass, the ball goes to the opposing team for a free pass restart.

(7.7)   When the ball or player carrying the ball, goes out of play, the ball goes to the team not responsible for taking the ball out of play for a free pass restart, at the point where the player or ball went out of play.

(7.8)   A player must not hand off or fend off an opponent in any way. (A free pass restart.)
          Note: players are recommended to carry the ball in two hands.

(7.9)   A player may not kick the ball. If this happens, possession goes to the opposing team at the point of kick for a free pass restart.

(7.10)   After a try has been scored, the game restarts from the centre with a free pass (as in 3 above).

(7.11)   A game will be made up of two halves each of up to 10 minutes' duration. During the interval coaches should take adequate time to talk to, encourage, coach and explain the game to the players. During the game coaches can direct and develop play in a coaching sense from on the field of play, ideally behind their teams.

Instructions:

(1)   At this age, a few inter-club games may take place, but certainly *not* more than five fixtures and one festival in any one season.

(2)   The emphasis should be on enjoyment. The children should be encouraged to enjoy the physical skills of running, passing, evasion and coached according to the material available in the 'Start Rugby' pack.

(3)   A coaching session should last no longer than 60 minutes with *no* more than 20 minutes devoted to match play.
          Note: in this version of the game there is a total emphasis on running with the ball, evasion, running in support of the ball carrier, passing, and running to touch the ball carrier.

In this version of the game there is:
          No tackling
          No scrummage
          No line-out
          No kicking

No hand off/fend off (*Note:* a hand off or fend off is defined as any movement of the hand or arm to ward off a would-be tackler.)

NON-CONTACT MINI RUGBY UNDER EIGHT

Key Stage 2

(8.1)   The object of the game is to score a try (5 points) by placing the ball with downward pressure on or behind the opponent's goal line.

(8.2)   The game is played between teams of not more than seven players.

(8.3)   The game is started or restarted with a free pass from the centre of the field. The starter's team must be behind the ball (i.e., nearer their own try line than the starter). The opposing team must be 7 metres away nearer its own goal line.

   Note: at a free pass the ball is held in two hands and is passed to a team member. The ball must be passed through the air and not taken from the hands of the first player. At every free pass restart (throughout all the games until U11) the passer must not run with the ball and he must not dummy pass. Normal play restarts as the pass is made.

(8.4)   The ball can ONLY be passed backwards or sideways, but not forwards.

   Note: the first receiver of a 'free pass' restart should start from no more than 2 metres behind the passer.

(8.5)   If a player running with the ball is touched with two hands below the waist by an opponent, the player must pass the ball as soon as possible and certainly within three strides. Opponents must not prevent the passer from passing the ball.

   Note: the three-stride rule is not intended to allow a player to continue to score a try, but if a player in the act of scoring a try is legally touched a try shall be awarded.

   Note: it is helpful for the referee to indicate that a 'Tackle' has been made, i.e., that the player has been touched, by shouting 'Tackled'.

(8.6)   When a team loses possession of the ball, it must retire 7 metres behind the point of restart on the line parallel to the goal line.

(8.7)   If a player – legally touched – fails to pass, the ball goes to the opposing team for a free pass restart.

(8.8)   When the ball, or player carrying the ball, goes out of play, the game restarts with a free pass at the point where the player or ball went out of play. The ball goes to the team not responsible for taking the ball out of play. The team without the ball must retire as for a free pass restart (*see* 3 above).

(8.9)   A player must not hand off or fend off an opponent in any way. (A free pass restart.)
         Note: players are recommended to carry the ball in two hands.

(8.10)   A player may not kick the ball. If this happens, it goes to the opposing team at the point of kick (a free pass restart).

(8.11)   After a try has been scored, the game restarts from the centre with a free pass (as in 3 above).

(8.12)   A game will be made up of two halves each of up to 10 minutes' duration. During the interval coaches should take adequate time to talk to, encourage, coach and explain the game to the players. During the game coaches can direct and develop play in a coaching sense from on the field of play, ideally behind their teams.

Instructions:

(1)   At this age players may play a maximum of one fixture every three weeks and not more than three festivals in any season. The emphasis remains on providing the children with an enjoyable introduction to the skills of the game. Competition is of secondary importance.

(2)   As the end of the season approaches (but NOT before 1 February), the concept of the set piece play of scrummage and back line may be introduced with all players experiencing all positions. Introduce the 'Chicken Scratch' scrum (uncontested) as illustrated in the RFU *A Coaching Guide to Mini-Rugby* video before progressing to a three-player uncontested scrummage. The scrummage will be made up of one row of three players from each team. The ball is put into the scrummage as laid down in the Laws of the Game of Rugby Football Union. The centre player of the three in the non-offending team sweeps the ball back through the legs of the player on his or her left with the right foot. The players of the offending team in the scrummage must not attempt to hook the ball or push their opponents backwards.

       The back line in the team not putting the ball into the scrummage must remain 7 metres behind the scrummage until normal play restarts, with the exception of the scrum half who must remain behind the hindmost foot of the forwards until normal play restarts. Normal play will restart when the ball has emerged from the scrummage.

(3)   A coaching session should last no longer than 60 minutes, with no more than 20 minutes devoted to match play.

(4)   On match days against outside opposition, a coaching session should normally precede the match. Matches should be used as an extension of the coaching session, with the emphasis being on the quality of performance rather than the result.

In this version of the game there is:

No tackling

No line-out

No kicking

No hand off/fend off

No scrummage until February, when Chicken Scratch or uncontested three-player scrum may be introduced.

MINI RUGBY UNDER NINE

Key Stage 2

(9.1)   The object of the game is to score a try (5 points) by placing the ball with downward pressure on or behind the opponent's goal line.

(9.2)   The game is played between teams of nine players, three of whom will form the scrummage, six of whom will form the back line. Positions should be interchangeable.

(9.3)   The game is started or restarted after a score with a free pass from the centre of the field. The starter's team must be behind the ball (i.e., nearer their own try line than the starter). The opposing team must be 7 metres away nearer its own goal line.

Note: at a free pass the ball is held in two hands and is passed to a team member. The ball must be passed through the air and not taken from the hands of the first player. At every free pass restart (throughout all the games until U11) the passer must not run with the ball and must not dummy pass.

Note: the first receiver of a 'free pass' restart should start from no more than 2 metres behind the passer.

(9.4)   The ball can ONLY be passed backwards or sideways.

(9.5)   If the ball is passed forward or knocked on, an uncontested scrummage is awarded.

(9.6)   Any player who is running with the ball can be tackled as laid down in the Laws of the Game.

(9.7)   If the ball is not playable IMMEDIATELY after a tackle, an uncontested scrummage is awarded to the team not in possession before the tackle.

Note: the referee should encourage tackler and tackled player to get away from the ball IMMEDIATELY so that the game can continue. Where a ruck or maul occurs, the off-side line for players not in the ruck or maul is at the hindmost foot on their side of the ruck or maul.

(9.8)   The scrummage will be made up of one row of three players *and no more* from each team. The team not responsible for the stoppage will put the ball into the scrummage and must be allowed to win it without contest. (Opponents cannot push or strike for the ball.) With these exceptions the Laws of the Game pertaining to the scrummage will apply.

(9.9)   The back line of the team not putting the ball into the scrummage must remain 7 metres behind the scrummage until normal play resumes, with the exception of the scrum half, who must remain behind the hindmost foot of his or her forwards until the ball emerges.

(9.10)   Normal play will restart when the ball has emerged from the scrummage.

(9.11)   When the ball, or player carrying the ball, goes out of the field of play, the game restarts with a free pass – 7 metres from touch on the line-of-touch (*see* Laws of the Game). The team without the ball must retire 7 metres from the line-of-touch. The ball goes to the team not responsible for taking the ball out of play.

(9.12)   After a try has been scored, the game restarts from the centre with a free pass (as in 9.3 above).

(9.13)   A player must not hand off or fend off an opponent in any way.

(9.14)   Following an infringement for:
          off side
          high or late tackle
          obstruction
          hand off/fend off
          kicking
          scrum feeding, striking for the ball and pushing
             in the scrummage
          a free pass restart ensues. The offending team must retire 7 metres from the point of restart, towards their own goal line.

(9.15)   A game will be made up of two halves of not more than 15 minutes' duration. During the interval coaches should take adequate time to talk to, encourage, coach and explain the game to the players.

Instructions:

(1)   Tackling must be introduced progressively, using the stages described in *Even Better Rugby*. (RFU Publication p 45–50 available from the RFU shop.)

(2)   The formation of the scrummage must be introduced in a progressive way following the stages described in *Even Better Rugby* with great emphasis placed on body position, foot placement, binding, putting the ball into the scrummage and hooking techniques.

(3)   At this age players may play a maximum of one fixture every three weeks and not more than three festivals in any season. The emphasis remains on providing the children with an enjoyable introduction to the skills of the game. Competition is of secondary importance.

(4)   A coaching session should normally last no longer than 60 minutes, with no more than 20 minutes devoted to match play.

(5)   On match days against outside opposition, a coaching session should normally precede the match. Matches should be used as an extension of the coaching session, with the emphasis being on the quality of performance rather than the result.

In this version of the game there is:
No line-out
No kicking
No hand off/fend off

MINI RUGBY UNDER TEN
Key Stage 2

(10.1)   The object of the game is to score a try (5 points) by placing the ball with downward pressure on or behind the opponent's goal line.

(10.2)   The game is played between teams of nine players, three of whom *and no more* will form the scrummage, six of whom will form the back line. Positions should be interchangeable.

(10.3)   The game is started or restarted after a score with a free pass from the centre of the field or 22-metre equivalent. The starter's team must be behind the ball (i.e. nearer their own try line than the starter). The opposing team must be 7 metres away nearer its own goal line.

         Note: at a free pass the ball is held in two hands and is passed to a team member. The ball must be passed through the air and not taken from the hands of the first player. At every free pass restart (throughout all the games until U11) the passer must not run with the ball and must not dummy pass.

Note: the first receiver of a free pass restart should start from no further than 2 metres behind the passer.

(10.4)   The ball can ONLY be passed backwards or sideways.

(10.5)   If the ball is passed forward or knocked on, a contested scrummage is awarded.

(10.6)   Any player who is running with the ball can be tackled as laid down in the Laws of the Game.

(10.7)   If the ball is not playable IMMEDIATELY after a tackle, a contested scrummage is awarded to the team not in possession before the tackle.

Note: the referee should encourage tackler and tackled player to get away from the ball IMMEDIATELY so that play can continue. Where a ruck or maul occurs, the off-side line for players not in the ruck or maul is at the hindmost foot on their side of the ruck or maul.

(10.8)   The scrummage will be made up of one row of three players *and no more* from each team. The team not responsible for the stoppage will put the ball into the scrummage. All the Laws of the Game pertaining to the U19 scrummage and including off side will apply except that the scrum half of the team not putting in the ball must remain behind the hindmost foot of the forwards until normal play restarts.

Normal play will restart when the ball has emerged from the scrummage. In the event of a strike against the head, the scrum half who has put the ball into the scrummage must not follow the ball until it is out of the scrummage.

(10.9)   If the ball, or player carrying the ball, goes out of play, a line-out (contested) at the point at which the ball or players crossed the touch-line will take place.

(10.10)   The line-out will be made up of no more than two players from each team plus the player throwing the ball in and an immediate opponent who must stand within the 2-metre area, and one player from either side in a position to receive the ball (i.e. scrum half).

(10.11)   The line-out will extend from 2 to 7 metres from the touch line.

(10.12)   The team not responsible for taking the ball out of play will throw the ball in.

(10.13)   The off side line for all players not participating in the line-out (all players other than those described under Rule 10.10 above) will be 7 metres back from the line of touch parallel to the goal line, and they must remain behind that off side line until the line-out has ended.
Note: see Laws of the Game for when line-out ends.

(10.14)   A player must not hand off or fend off an opponent in any way. Penalty: a free pass restart.
Note: players are recommended to carry the ball in two hands.

(10.15)   After a try has been scored, the game restarts from the centre with a free pass (as in 10.3 above).

(10.16)   Following an infringement for:
off side
high or late tackle
obstruction
hand off/fend off
kicking
scrum feeding
a free pass restart ensues as in 10.3 above.

(10.17)   A game will be made up of two halves each of not more than 15 minutes duration. During the interval coaches should take adequate time to talk to, encourage, coach and explain the game to the players.

Instructions:

(1)   At this age players may play not more than one fixture every three weeks and not more than three festivals in any season.

(2)   Coaching sessions which include talks, videos, etc., should not normally last longer than two hours, with a maximum of 30 minutes devoted to match play.

(3)   On match days against outside opposition, a coaching session should normally precede the game. The game should be used as an extension of the coaching session, with the emphasis on the quality of performance, rather than the result.

In this version of the game there is:
No kicking
No hand off/fend off

MINI RUGBY UNDER ELEVEN

Key Stage 2

(11.1)   The object of the game is to score a try (5 points) by placing the ball with downward pressure on or behind the opponent's goal line. A further 2 points are given for a successful conversion.

(11.2)   The game is played between teams of nine players, three of whom *and no more* will form the scrummage, six of whom will form the back line. Positions should be interchangeable.

(11.3)   At this age the game will start with a KICK-OFF from the centre of the field. The kicker's team must be behind the ball until it has been kicked and the receiving team must be at least 7 metres back from the ball.
    Note: read Senior Law if ball is kicked off directly into touch and In-goal.

(11.4)   The ball can ONLY be passed backwards or sideways.

(11.5)   If the ball is passed forward or knocked on, a contested scrummage is awarded.

(11.6)   Any player who is running with the ball can be tackled as laid down in the Laws of the Game.

(11.7)   If the ball is not playable IMMEDIATELY after a tackle, a scrummage is awarded to the team not in possession before the tackle.
    Note: The referee should encourage tackler and tackled player to get away from the ball IMMEDIATELY so that play can continue. Where a ruck or maul occurs, the off-side line for players not in the ruck or maul is at the hindmost foot on their side of the ruck or maul.

(11.8)   The scrummage will be made up of one row of three players *and no more* from each team. The team not responsible for the stoppage will put the ball into the scrummage. All the usual Laws of the Game pertaining to the U19 scrummage and including off side will apply except that the scrum half of the team not putting in the ball must remain behind the hindmost foot of the forwards until normal play restarts.
    Normal play will restart when the ball has emerged from the scrummage. In the event of a strike against the head, the scrum half who has put the ball into the scrummage must not follow the ball until it is out of the scrummage.

(11.9)   If the ball, or player carrying the ball, goes out of play, a line-out at the point at which the ball or players crossed the touch line will take place.

(11.9.1) The line-out will be made up of no more than two players from each team plus the player throwing the ball in and an immediate opponent who must stand within the 2-metre area, and one player from either side in a position to receive the ball (i.e. scrum half).

(11.9.2) The line-out will extend from 2 to 7 metres from the touch line.

(11.9.3) The team not responsible for taking the ball out of play will throw the ball in.

(11.10) The off-side line for all players not participating in the line-out (all players other than those described under Rule 11.9.1 above) will be 7 metres back from the line of touch parallel to the goal line, and they must remain behind that off-side line until the line-out has ended.

(11.11) A player must not hand off or fend off an opponent in any way (a free pass restart). The opposition must retire 7 metres towards their own goal line from the place where the free pass is awarded.
Note: players are recommended to carry the ball in two hands.

(11.12) All the Laws of the Game pertaining to kicking in open play apply except that players may not kick the ball in general play other than out of their hands.

(11.13) After a try has been scored, the team can attempt to convert the try into a goal. The kick at goal will take place from anywhere in front of the posts.

(11.14) After a try or goal has been scored the game will restart with a drop kick.

(11.15) When an infringement occurs as per the Laws of the Game a penalty or free-kick will be awarded. The opposition must retire at least 7 metres back towards their own goal line from the place where the kick is awarded.

(11.16) At this age, a game will be made up of two halves of not more than 15 minutes each. During the interval coaches should take adequate time to talk to, encourage, coach and explain the game to the players.

Instructions:

(1) At this age, players may play not more than one fixture every three weeks and not more than three festivals in any season.

(2) Coaching sessions which include talks, videos, etc., should not normally last longer than two hours, with a maximum of 30 minutes devoted to match play.

(3)   On match days against outside opposition, a coaching session should normally precede the game. The game should be used as an extension of the coaching session, with the emphasis on the quality of performance, rather than the result.

In this version of the game there is:
   No hand off/fend off

MIDI RUGBY UNDER TWELVE

Key Stage 3

(12.1)   The object of the game is to score a try (5 points) by placing the ball with downward pressure on or behind the opponent's goal line.

(12.2)   Teams will be made up of twelve players, five forwards *and no more* and seven backs.

The Laws of the Game of Rugby Football Union apply with the following exceptions.

(12.3)   SCRUMMAGE:
   (a)   The locks forming the second row must bind to each other with their inside arm and with their outside arm around the hips of the front row (props).
   (b)   The scrum half not putting the ball in must remain behind the off side line (the hindmost foot) until the ball has emerged from the scrummage. In the event of a strike against the head, the scrum half who has put the ball into the scrummage must not follow the ball until it is out.
   (c)   See Laws of the Game, the Experimental Laws 1993/94 including U19 Laws for the 1993/94 Season.

(12.4)   LINE-OUT:
   (a)   The line-out will be made up of two, three or four players from each side plus the player throwing the ball in and the latter's immediate opponent who must stand within the 2-metre area, and one player from either side in a position to receive the ball (i.e. scrum half).
   (b)   The line-out will extend from 2 to 7 metres from the touch line.
   (c)   See the Laws of the Game, the Experimental Laws 1993/94 including U19 Laws for the 1993/94 Season.

(12.5)   A player must not hand off or fend off an opponent in any way (a free kick restart – the opposition must retire 7 metres towards their

own goal line from the place where the free kick is awarded).
Note: players are recommended to carry the ball in two hands.

(12.6)   A game will be made up of two equal halves of not more
         than 20 minutes each. During the interval coaches should take
         adequate time to talk to, encourage, coach and explain the game
         to players.

Instructions:

(1)   At this age no more than one fixture should be played in every
      two weeks and not more than three festivals in any season.

(2)   If there are insufficient numbers to play MIDI RUGBY (U12)
      they should play MINI RUGBY still in their U12 age group.

(3)   On match days against outside opposition, a coaching session
      (30–35 minutes) should normally precede the game. The game
      should be used as an extension of the coaching session, with the
      result seen to be less important than the QUALITY of performance.

(4)   A practical coaching session that includes talks and videos, etc.,
      should last no longer than 2 hours with a maximum of 40 minutes
      devoted to match play.

In this version of the game there is:
   No hand off/fend off

For further information consult:

The Coaching Guide to Mini-Rugby (Video)
Even Better Rugby (Publication and Video)
'Mini Rugby Directive' – Revised May 1992 to be found in the RFU
1993/94 Handbook and Laws of the Game.

NEW IMAGE RUGBY

For the junior schools of England where mixed classes are the norm and
where children play together, the New Image Rugby (non-contact) has been
enthusiastically embraced by both teachers and pupils.
   The basic rules and key points are as follows:

(1)   New Image is a game designed for any number of players. It is a
      fast and exciting (non-contact) team game of two-handed touch
      played by boys and girls, mums and dads, with the added bonus
      that all can play in the same game at the same time on the same
      pitch.

(2)   Points (5) may only be gained by scoring a try. The way to score a try is to press the ball down over the opponent's try-line with both hands.

(3)   The game is started with a free pass from the halfway line. The passer's team must be behind the ball (i.e., nearer to their own try line than the ball). Opponents should be at least 7 metres away.

(4)   The size of the pitch and the duration of the play rather depends on the age and ability of the participants.

(5)   At a free pass the opponents must be 7 metres away from the free pass on a line running parallel to the goal line.

(6)   There is no tackling. Defenders must touch the ball carrier with two hands simultaneously, one hand on either side of the ball carrier's hips. The ball carrier must then pass the ball immediately (but not forward) to a team-mate.

(7)   Failure to do so results in a free pass being awarded to the opposition.

(8)   Offside. A player may only be offside on three particular occasions, namely at the free pass, a scrum or a line-out.

(9)   For the very young, one coach per side should be allowed on the pitch, but should remain behind the last player on his side while the game is in progress. The comments he makes should be constructive and given in a calm manner – hysteria is counter-productive.

(10)   If a player passes, knocks or drops the ball forward and it touches the ground a scrum shall be awarded.

(11)   To take a free pass a player from the non-offending team picks up the ball and passes to a team-mate.

(12)   Remember opponents at least 7 metres away.

(13)   Player may run with the ball but must not pass forward (i.e., towards the opponent's try-line).

(14)   The line-out is formed by five forwards from each team. Four forwards from each team stand in Indian file facing the touch-line. The fifth forward throws in the ball from the touch-line between the two lines of forwards. One of the team-mates of the thrower-in must jump and catch the ball above head height and be bound by the two players on either side.

(15)   Opponents may do nothing until the scrum half of the opposing team has the ball. If the team throwing in the ball fails to jump and catch the ball at the first attempt, a second attempt should

be allowed. Thereafter, the opposition are awarded a free pass from anywhere within the length of the line-out.

(16)   At scrums and line-outs all players other than the forwards and the scrum half must be 7 metres back from the mid line of the scrum and/or line-out; this offside line is an imaginary line which stretches right across the pitch.

(17)   If the ball crosses the touch-line, play is restarted by a line-out with the ball thrown in by a member of the team which did not cause the ball to go out of play.

(18)   The scrum contains five players, three in the front row, two in the second with heads placed as per diagram below for twelve-a-side and eleven-a-side. No pushing is allowed and the opposition cannot strike for the ball. The scrum half stands on the left-hand side of his own team's scrum and holds the ball in two hands midway between the knee and ankle and puts the ball in straight.

12 A-SIDE

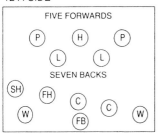

11 A-SIDE

10 A-SIDE

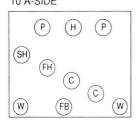

9 A-SIDE

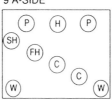

8 A-SIDE

7 A-SIDE

6 A-SIDE

5 A-SIDE

4 A-SIDE

3 A-SIDE

IRELAND
LEPRECHAUN RUGBY
LAWS FOR LEPRECHAUN RUGBY

Leprechaun Rugby has been developed to introduce the game of Rugby Union to primary-school children. It has been designed to develop the skills of running, ball handling and a form of tackling which does not make ground contact. Rugby Union scrums and line-outs are included. As the forceful contest is removed from these set plays, the options and opportunities for running players are increased.

The non-tackling and soft-contact nature of Leprechaun Rugby contains all the running and handling skills of Rugby Union and allows boys and girls, and players of different ages and sizes, to play safely together.

The lessons include practices designed to promote co-operation and decision-making. The drills concentrate on skills and co-ordination which will help in the general development of any young player.

PLAYING FIELD OR AREA

This can be any size from 10 m × 20 m upwards, i.e. four-a-side game can play on 10 × 20 m area. Eight-a-side game can play on a 30 m × 40 m area. Twelve-a-side can play on a 50 m × 70 m area.

NUMBER OF PLAYERS

This can vary from four-a-side up to twelve-a-side. The emphasis is always on having more backs than forwards. Suggested format for the number of players a-side could be:

Four-a-side game: 1-person scrum, 1-person line-out, 3 backs.
Eight-a-side game: 3-person scrum, 2-person line-out, 5 backs.
Twelve-a-side game: 5-person scrum, 4-person line-out, 7 backs.

DURATION

This will depend on the time available, the age of the players and the numbers involved in each team. For example, suggested times:

Four-a-side: 5 minutes each way then rotate teams.
Eight-a-side: 10 minutes each way.
Twelve-a-side: 15 minutes each way.

If competitions are being organized Leprechaun Laws must apply and times should be specified by the organizers.

SCORING

5 points are awarded for tries. A try is scored by pressing the ball down over the try line with one or both hands.

START OF PLAY

The team who wins the toss can either choose the end of the pitch or to pass/kick off. When passing/kicking off the opposition must be 5–10 metres away depending on the size of the pitch and the size of the teams.

OFFSIDE

In Leprechaun Rugby there is no offside when running, tagging and passing. However, offside lines apply for set plays (scrum and line-out) and the ball take. These are imaginary lines drawn across the field parallel to the goal lines.

ATTACKING TEAM

The attacking team carries the ball downfield, running, passing or handing back, to score a try by placing the ball over the goal line. The ball can only be transferred to a player behind the ball carrier. No forward handling or passing is allowed.

DEFENDING TEAM

The defending team attempts to halt the running progress of the attacking team by tagging the ball carrier.

TAGGING AND BALL TAKE

To tag, a player must contact the ball carrier with two hands (one on each side of the hips). The ball carrier must then immediately pass backwards. Any attempt to gain territory without trying to pass, will result in loss of possession.

Or, if the ball carrier can't see anyone to pass to, he/she should immediately stop, turn and transfer the ball to a support player. The support player must then pass the ball without running.

LEPRECHAUN LINE-OUT

If the ball, or player carrying the ball, crosses the touch-line, play is restarted by a line-out with the ball thrown in by a member of the non-offending team.

The line-out can be formed in:

Four-a-side game: 1 forward from each team.
Eight-a-side game: 2 forwards from each team.
Twelve-a-side game: 4 forwards from each team.

The forwards from each team stand in file facing the touch-line. In the twelve-a-side game the fifth forward not in the line-out throws in the ball from the touch-line between the two lines of forwards. The opposite fifth forward must remain beside the thrower. One of the team-mates of the thrower must jump and catch the ball above head height and can be bound by one player on either side. There is a half-metre gap between the players in each line. No player from either side can leave the line-out until the ball is in the hands of the scrum half. If a team throwing in the ball fails to jump and catch the first attempt, a second attempt should be allowed. After that the opposition are awarded a penalty anywhere within the length of the line-out.

At line-outs all players other than forwards and the scrum halves must be 5 metres back from the mid line of the line-out. This offside line is an imaginary line and stretches right across the pitch.

INTERCEPTING THE BALL

An opposition pass may be intercepted.

GATHERING A DROPPED BALL

If the attacking team drops, knocks or throws the ball to the ground, the defending team can pick up the ball and play on. If the attacking team picks up the ball a scrum is formed, with the defending team putting the ball into the scrum.

FORWARD PASS

A forward pass is an infringement, and when this occurs a scrum takes place with the non-infringing side putting the ball into the scrum.

GOAL LINE TAGS

When a ball carrier is tagged over any goal line, a scrum is formed 5 metres in from the goal line with the tagger's team putting the ball into the scrum.

LEPRECHAUN SCRUM

(1)   A scrum occurs when:

    (a)   A player drops the ball forward and a player from the same side picks it up.

    (b)   A forward pass is made.

    (c)   The player accidentally becomes involved in play while offside.

    (d)   The player with the ball is tagged behind the goal line.

(2)   The scrum can consist of 1–5 players, for example:
four-a-side game: 1 player from each side in the scrum.
Eight-a-side game: 3 players from each side in the scrum.
Twelve-a-side game: 5 players from each side in the scrum.

(3)   In the twelve-a-side game the scrum consists of five players, three in the front row and two in the second row. *No pushing* is permitted and the opposition may not contest for the ball. The scrum half stands on the left-hand side of the scrum, holds the ball midway between knee and ankle and puts the ball in straight. Then it is struck (won) by a team-mate in the hooking position so that the ball comes out the back of the scrum where the scrum half will either pass or run with it. The opposing scrum half must be positioned behind the scrum and must not move from there until the ball emerges from the scrum.

PENALTIES

All penalties are tap kicks. A player from the non-offending team simply taps the ball on the ground and passes to a team-mate. All opposing players must be at least 5 metres from where the kick is taken.

REASONS FOR AWARDING PENALTIES

(1)   Ball carrier pushes or hands off opponent.

(2)   Defending player prevents the ball carrier from passing or transferring the ball immediately after a tackle.

(3)   The ball carrier makes further ground after a tackle, without passing the ball.

(4)   A player in a scrum or line-out competes for the ball when his/her team is not putting the ball in.

(5)   A player in the opposing team takes the ball from the ball carrier.

(6)   A player deliberately obstructs an opponent.

(7)   A player is offside.

SAFETY IN LEPRECHAUN RUGBY

The modified laws (no tackling or pushing in scrums) enable children to play in a variety of positions, learn the running and passing skills of a back-line player as well as the positioning, tactics and skills of a forward player.

Playing sport places physical demands on children, and the teaching of skills and laws in preparation for competition is essential for satisfying and safe participation.

SCRUM SAFETY

In a scrum, children with long, thin necks are not suitable for the front and second rows of scrums and *must not be selected* to play in these positions. Even though the laws of Leprechaun Rugby have been modified to exclude pushing, the principle of selecting appropriate body types starts at this level.

Front-row players should always be of similar size. A balance within the second row unit is also recommended.

Players in the scrum should always keep their head up and above the height of their hips.

When an injured player leaves the field, particular attention must be given to the physique of the replacement player. It may be necessary to reallocate playing positions.

AFTER LEPRECHAUN RUGBY – WHAT NEXT?

Mini Rugby has been the very successful basic introductory game for the code since the sixties. Players learn the important aspect of Rugby Union, such as the value of support, how to use space and how to combine with other members of the team.

Like Leprechaun Rugby, players become well-versed in the fundamentals of running and ball handling. However, Mini Rugby introduces physical contact which can occur when stopping the ball carrier with a tackle, contesting the ball after a tackle, and in the scrum.

Mixed Mini Rugby has been played for many years in the pre-puberty age group where contact is not a problem between boys and girls. At that level of maturation, very little power can be developed. Beyond that, however, the game should be restricted to all male or female groups. This situation has been a part of senior Rugby Union in many countries.

SCOTLAND

STAGES OF DEVELOPMENT
NEW IMAGE RUGBY

This game will continue to be promoted as a primary school class activity. It is proving increasingly popular as such.

It will also be used at club level as a supplement to Mini Rugby. It can have positive input at any level.

MINI RUGBY
Primary 4, 5, 6 and 7 Year Groups

The S.R.U. does not actively promote any form of structured game for children below the primary 4 age group. Where a sufficient number of such children arrive at a club they should be encouraged to develop their own 'game' within a supervised, rather than a controlled, situation.

ALIGNMENT OF CLUB AGE GROUPINGS
WITH SCHOOL YEAR GROUPS

Player Group	Rugby Classification	School Equivalent	Game Format	Team Organization
All Children in Primary 4	P4	Primary 4	8 a-side	3 man front row 5 backs
All Children in Primary 5	P5	Primary 5	8 a-side	3 man front row 5 backs
All Children in Primary 6	P6	Primary 6	8 a-side	3 man front row 5 backs
All Children in Primary 7	P7	Primary 7	10 a-side	5 forwards 5 backs

[P4, P5 and P6 Rugby]

These three age groups will play eight-a-side Mini Rugby as it is currently played with the following Law amendments:

(1)   The scrum will be formed by three forwards from each team viz: prop, hooker, prop.

(2)   There will be NO PUSHING OR WHEELING OF THE SCRUM. Any scrum which wheels shall be reformed or a penalty awarded if the referee considers the wheel deliberate.

(3)   At each scrum both hookers should attempt to strike for the ball.

(4)   At all scrums and 'tap and pass' restarts, the scrum half *must* pass the ball. He may, however, run with it in open play.

(5)   General Play – In OPEN PLAY the team in possession is responsible for the continuity of play, therefore, if play is stopped in a ruck/maul situation, possession will go to the opposing team and the game restarted with a 'tap and pass'.

(6)   After a try has been scored, the team losing the try will restart the game with a 'tap and pass' at the centre of the field.

It is recommended that the game at P4, P5 and P6 will be two halves of 10 minutes.

Note: Referees must emphasise the OFF-SIDE LAWS at set piece and restart situations; taking time to explain decisions where obvious confusion exists.

[P7 Rugby]

It is at this age group that the first progression is introduced. It will still be called Mini Rugby.

(1)   The game will be played ten-a-side (five forwards, five backs).

(2)   The scrum will be formed viz:

       Prop   Hooker   Prop

          Lock   Lock

(3)   There will be NO PUSHING IN THE SCRUM and both hookers must strike for the ball.

(4)   Wheeling of the scrum is *not* permitted. A scrum which wheels will be reformed *or* a penalty awarded if the referee deems it to be deliberate.

(5)   The scrum half must pass the ball after a scrum and at other restarts.

(6)   When the ball goes over the side-line the game will be restarted with a line-out as follows:

    (a)   All the forwards will be involved in each line-out. One to throw in, or mark the thrower, the others forming the line-out, approximately 3–5 metres from the touch-line.

    (b)   Only the players of the team throwing in are allowed to jump for the ball. The first player to play the ball must attempt to have both feet off the ground and hands above head height (Penalty – FREE KICK).

    (c)   The forwards of the non-throwing in team may *not* contest for the ball until it has been played:

        (i)   They may not jump for the ball.

        (ii)   They must keep their hands below head height.

        (iii)   They must not interfere with any player in the opposition team until the ball has been played.

    (d)   The scrum half *must* pass the ball when it emerges from the line-out (Penalty – FREE KICK).

    (e)   All backs (except the scrum half) must remain 10 metres back from the line of touch until the ball has emerged from the line-out or has been deflected from the line of touch (Penalty – PENALTY KICK).

(7)   General Play – In OPEN PLAY, the team in possession is responsible for the continuity of play, therefore, if play is stopped in a ruck/maul situation, possession will go to the opposing team and the game restarted with a free kick.

The recommended time for games at this level is three sessions of 10 minutes (the final session can be split in cases where weather/ground advantage is thought to be significant).

The pitch size is recommended as touch-line to touch-line using goal line to 10-metre line for width. This will allow two matches to be played simultaneously on one full-sized pitch. Obvious care must be taken to protect posts and the playing area can be suitably flagged to avoid the posts intruding on to the pitch.

Note for Coaches/Teachers

In view of:

(1)   the extra space available;
(2)   the requirement of the scrum half to pass;
and
(3)   the restriction on kicking to within 5 metres of own goal line,

the practice of passing, pick-up, and running skills will require special attention. These skills must be practised regularly, both in isolation and within game-based activities.

WALES
DRAGON RUGBY
RULES

The following are suggested rules for *Inter-School Matches*.

Numbers are not the most important thing but nine-a-side is ideal with the formation of four forwards (two in the front row) and five backs, since the progression then to Mini Rugby is easier and the players will understand all the positions.

Field of Play

The game can be played anywhere but the size of the field should correspond to the number of players.

Number of Players

Ideal number: nine to four forwards (two in the front row) five backs.

Playing Time

10-minute spells with 2 minutes' half-time break.

Size of Ball

Dragon Ball or if not available size 3.

THE GAME

(1)   Play is continuous, only stopping when:
    (a)   Points are scored.
    (b)   Infringements occur.
    (c)   Ball goes out of play.

(2)   Advantage should be played as often as possible.

(3)   There is no kicking apart from a conversion and tap penalty.

(4)   The game is about catching, passing, running, support and team-play.

KICK-OFF

(1)   A tap kick is taken from the centre of the halfway line by the team starting each half of the game and by the team which has just had a try scored against it.

(2)   The receiving team must stand 10 metres from the halfway line.

METHOD OF SCORING

(1)   A try is scored when the ball is grounded on or over the try line.

(2)   If posts are available to convert a try, the ball can be kicked in any fashion over the cross bar by any member of the try-scoring team from a position in front of the goal posts.

(3)   The opposing team stand still under the goal posts until after the conversion attempt.

LINE-OUT

(1)   A line-out is awarded when:
    (a)   The ball lands on or over the touch-line.
    (b)   A player carrying the ball puts a foot on or over the touch-line.

(2)   Formation
    (a)   The line-out takes place 3 metres from the touch-line.
    (b)   The forwards must form the line-out.
    (c)   The forwards must stand a metre from each other and a half-metre from their opponents.

(3)   Throwing in the ball
    (a)   The team throwing in the ball must win the ball.
    (b)   The catcher must jump to catch the ball above the head.
    (c)   If the ball is not caught then the opposition is awarded a tap penalty 10 metres out from where the ball went into touch.

(4)   Restriction on players
        (a)   All players not in the line-out must be 10 metres back
                from the line-out.
        (b)   All players must remain still until the ball is in the
                scrum half's hands.

(5)   Quick throw-in
        (a)   A quick throw-in from touch without waiting for the
                players to form a line-out is *permissible and should be
                encouraged*, provided the same ball is used, has only been
                handled by the players and is thrown in straight – at least
                3 metres.

PENALTY

(1)   Advantage should always be played.
        (a)   All penalties are tap kicks.
        (b)   Tap kicks must be taken from the place of infringement.
        (c)   The kicker must kick the ball whilst it is on the ground.

(2)   Penalties are awarded for:
        (a)   A defending player preventing the ball carrier from passing.
        (b)   Holding, pulling or pushing the ball carrier.
        (c)   Ball carrier failing to pass or release the ball immediately
                after a tackle.
        (d)   An infringement at scrum or line-out.

(3)   Restriction on players
        (a)   The offending team must retire 10 metres from the
                mark until the ball is played, if not the penalty is
                moved forward 10 metres.
        (b)   The attacking team must be behind the ball when it
                is played, if not a scrum is given to the non-offending
                team.

TACKLE

(1)   A tackle is made when the defending player touches the ball
        carrier with two hands on the hips.

(2)   The ball carrier must immediately release or pass the ball after
        being tackled. The ball carrier must not attempt to make any
        further ground, but some forward momentum is permissible.

(3)   The referee should call 'pass' when the player is tackled.

(4)   Referees are to encourage players to pass the ball immediately
        once they are tackled rather than wait for 'pass' to be called.

THE SCRUM

(1)   A scrum is awarded when:

(a)   A player fumbles the ball and it travels forwards towards the opponent's goal line and has not been recovered before it touches the ground.

(b)   A player throws or passes the ball forward. However, if the opposition gain advantage then play should continue.

(2)   Formation

(a)   Four or more players.

(b)   The prop(s) and the hooker bind around each other by placing their hands around the mid-section of the body.

(c)   Players place their hands and shoulders on the left hand side of the player opposite them in the scrum so that the front rows interlock.

(3)   Putting the ball into the scrum

(a)   The scrum half puts the ball into the scrum from the left-hand side.

(b)   The ball must touch the ground first before being played.

(4)   Restriction on players

(a)   No player must push in the scrum.

(b)   Only the hooker of the team putting in the ball must strike for the ball.

(c)   The scrum half of the side *not putting in the ball* must stand directly behind his own scrum.

(d)   All other players must be 10 metres back from the scrum.

(e)   No player can move until the ball is out of the scrum.

AUSTRALIA
WALLA RUGBY
PHILOSOPHY OF COACHING AND REFEREEING
JUNIOR RUGBY

Walla Rugby is a simple game designed to provide the initial introduction to the skills and concepts of rugby and to act as Step One of the Australian Junior Rugby Pathway.

The essential feature of Junior Rugby is one of enjoyment. As such, a purely technical refereeing approach to the application of the laws of Walla Rugby could be contrary to the spirit of the game.

Walla Rugby should be free-flowing with the purpose of developing the skills of running, balance and ball handling, as well as establishing the concept of set plays through the modified scrum, maul and line-out situations. At all times safety must be a paramount consideration whilst coaching and refereeing the game.

It is recommended that at all times referees adopt an *encouraging and educative*, rather than punitive, whistle-happy approach.

The desirable qualities of rugby – sportsmanship and fair play – should be positively rewarded. This may be done by the quiet word or open comment, rather than penalty.

Of course, any dangerous action by a player should be quickly and firmly dealt with, but again the emphasis should be on an educative approach.

Coaches must ensure that the skills of the game are correctly taught and that the success achieved by each player is acknowledged and encouraged. It is vital that each and every player receives the same opportunity to develop in an environment of friendliness and co-operation. Satisfaction should be gained from participation, improvement and competitive performance – without the emphasis on win at all costs.

The concept of positive reinforcement of the ideals of the game and skills of players cannot be over-emphasized. Unlike the more senior levels of rugby, where the referee's role is to interpret, judge and decide, Walla Rugby requires a different philosophy by the referee and coach.

It is also strongly recommended that the emphasis on competition at this age level be minimized. Players should be left to develop skills and learn the game without the presence of external pressure to 'win premierships'.

Accordingly, there should be no finals series, no competition table and no premiership awarded at this age level.

In summary:

> keep it simple, free-flowing and enjoyable;
> let the players develop skills, with safety;
> discourage any dangerous action or unsafe practice;
> adopt an educative, positive reinforcement approach;
> ensure that players receive an equal opportunity to participate, regardless of ability.

SUMMARY OF THE FEATURES OF WALLA RUGBY FOR UNDER 7/8 YEAR OLDS AS STEP ONE OF THE AUSTRALIAN JUNIOR RUGBY PATHWAY

(1)   Playing Area: Maximum 69 m × 35 m (across full field from 5-metre to 40-metre line) *Note:* 69 m × 22 m – across one quarter field is also most acceptable.

(2)   Team Size: Ten players per standard team.

(3)   Ball Size: Size 3 (Walla Rugby) football recommended for this age group.

(4)   Playing Time: Two 15-minute halves.

(5)   Scoring: A try is worth 5 points. No goal kicking at this age level.

(6)   Kick-off: Must travel 5 metres towards the opponent's goal line.

(7)   Kicking in General Play: No kicking is allowed in general play.

(8)   Drop-outs: Taken from the line 15 metres out from the goal line.

(9)   Fair Catch: There is no fair-catch 'Mark' provision at this age level.

(10)   Penalty Kick: The 'Tap Kick' is the only option for a team receiving a penalty. The defending team must stand back 5 metres towards their own goal line.

(11)   Walla Tag: To halt the progress of the ball carrier a defending player must contact the ball carrier with two hands (simultaneously) below waist height.
       Once tagged the ball carrier has two options:
       (a)   Pass the ball to a team-mate immediately;
       (b)   Set up for a ball take.

(12)   Scrum: Three-player scrum with all three in the front row. There is no pushing in a Walla Scrum. Only the hooker may strike for the ball.

(13)   Line-out: Maximum four-player line-out. The ball is thrown in to the line standing 3 metres from touch. Back lines back 5 metres from the line of touch.

(14)   Advantage: Referees should play the advantage law generously to ensure a free-flowing game.

(15)   Offside: There is no offside in general play. Offside lines exist for scrum, line-out and ball-take situations (see relevant sections).

(16)   Finals Series: No finals, no competition ladder and no premiership awarded at this age level.

AUSTRALIAN JUNIOR RUGBY PATHWAY
Step One

Under 7–8   Walla Rugby
               (Ten-a-side)
               (Non-Tackling – No Kicking)

Step Two

Under 9–10   Mini Rugby
               (Ten-a-side – introduction to contact)

Step Three

Under 11–12   Midi Rugby
               (Twelve-a-side – stepping stone to full game)

Step Four

Under 13–19   Under 19 Laws
               (Fifteen-a-side)

NEW ZEALAND

My opposite number in New Zealand is Lee Smith, Director of Coaching, and he tells me, 'We recommend nationally that New Image Rugby is played up to the under-nine level. We can say confidently that in schools New Image Rugby as part of the physical education programme is played up to eleven years of age. However, while we are sure that some New Image Rugby is played in all provinces the age group at which it is introduced can vary according to how enlightened the provincial union is.

'The only way we have found to ensure New Image Rugby is implemented is to automatically introduce it and put up with criticism for a transition period of two to three years until it becomes accepted.'

This situation has much in common with the situation in other traditional rugby countries. When the virtues of New Image (non-contact) are explained to educationalists they immediately see the logic and virtue of introducing rugby in a progressive and systematic way. In other words, in a manner appropriate to a growing child. On the other hand the non-teacher trained tends initially to see only the full-contact game as the way forward. Happily much of the animosity generated by the non-contact approach is behind all Unions and the game thrives.

THE LAWS OF NEW IMAGE RUGBY
KICKING-OFF

(1)   The game is started with a kick-off at the beginning of both the first and second halves and each time after a try is scored.

(2)   The kick is taken from the centre of the halfway line.

(3)   The kick may be a punt, drop kick or place kick depending on the age and skill level of the players.

(4)   The kicker's team must be behind the halfway line until the kick is taken.

(5)   At primary-school level the opposing team must be 5 metres away from the halfway line when the kick is taken; at secondary-school

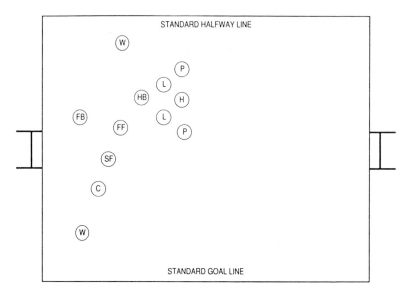

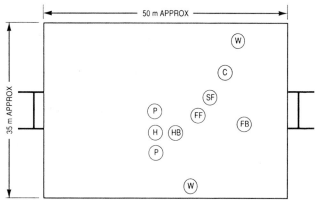

TEAM KEY (New Zealand terminology)

(H) HOOKER   (SH) SCRUM HALF

(P) PROP   (FH) FLY HALF

(L) LOCK

(C) CENTRE   (HB) HALF BACK

(W) WING   (FF) FIRST FIVE EIGHTH

(FB) FULL BACK   (SF) SECOND FIVE EIGHTH

level the opposing team must be 10 metres away from the halfway line when the kick is taken. The kick should reach the opposing team.

SCORING

(1) A try is scored by pressing the ball down over the goal line with one or two hands or arms or the player's torso.

(2) Five points are awarded for a try.

CONVERSIONS

(1) All conversion kicks at goal after a try are taken in front of the goal posts regardless of where the try was scored.

(2) These kicks may be place kicks, drop kicks or punt kicks, depending on the age and skill level of players.

(3) Two points are awarded for a conversion.

THE SCRUM
Numbers and Formation

(1) The scrum contains three or five players depending on the number of players in the team.

(2) If there are eleven or twelve players in a team a five-player scrum is formed.

(3) Where team numbers are ten players or less a three-player scrum is formed.

(4) A three-player scrum has a front row containing two props and a hooker.

(5) A five-player scrum has a front row and two locks.

Hooking the Ball

(1) At all levels below secondary school the hook is not contested. At secondary-school level the hook may be contested by the opposition hooker.

The Feed into the Scrum

(1) The half back feeds from the left-hand side of the scrum rolling the ball along the mid-line of the tunnel.

(2) Restrictions on players:
no pushing is allowed;

only the hooker can strike for the ball;

non-feeding half backs must stand directly behind their scrum;

the back lines must stand behind the hindmost foot of their scrums in a position to run and pass the ball;

the defensive back line cannot move until the ball is in the attacking half back's hands.

THE LINE-OUT
Numbers

(1)   The number of players in the line-out is the same as those involved in the scrum. The players are the same players as those participating in the scrum.

Formation

(1)   In a three-player line-out both props from each team stand facing the touch-line one behind the other. In a five-player line-out the props and the locks take up this formation.

(2)   There is a half-metre gap between the two lines and a metre gap between the players in each line.

The Throw-in

(1)   The hooker throws the ball in down the line of team-mates – if the players are too young the referee throws the ball in.

Variations

(1)   The distance from the touch-line to the players at the front of the line-out may vary from 3 to 5 metres depending on the age and skill level of players.

The Catch

(1)   The catch is uncontested in primary- and intermediate-school teams.

(2)   The ball is caught with the hands above the head in primary-school teams.

(3)   The ball is caught with the hands above the head and with the feet off the ground in intermediate-school teams. (The players jump and catch the ball.)

(4)   In secondary-school teams possession may be contested.

(5)   The hooker throws the ball down the centre line between the players and calls a position in the line-out to which the throw is

to be made. The player from each team in that position contests possession.

Restrictions on Players

(1) No player from either team may leave the line-out until the ball is in the hands of a half-back.

(2) At primary-school level both back lines stand 5 metres behind their respective sides of the line-out in a position to run and pass the ball. At secondary-school level both back lines stand 10 metres behind their respective sides of the line-out.

THE TACKLE

(1) To make a tackle the defender must place both hands on the ball carrier's hips – one on each side.

(2) The ball carrier must, before running a further 2 metres, pass the ball to a supporting player or place the ball on the ground.

PENALTY KICK

(1) All penalty kicks are tap kicks. A player from the non-offending team taps the ball along the ground, picks it up and must pass it back to a team-mate who initiates the attack.

Reasons for Awarding a Penalty

(1) Fending or pushing an opponent.

(2) A defending player preventing the ball carrier passing the ball immediately following a tackle.

(3) The ball carrier running more than 2 metres after being tackled before passing or releasing the ball.

(4) A player in a scrum or line-out competing for the ball when their team is not putting it into the scrum or line-out – except secondary-school players.

(5) A player in the defending team taking the ball from the ball carrier.

(6) When a player is in an offside position in general play and interfering with the continuity of play.

OFFSIDE

(1) In general play players are in an offside position when they are in front of the ball when it was last played by a team-mate.

KNOCK-ON, FORWARD PASS

If a player:

> knocks or drops the ball forward and it touches the ground;

> or passes the ball forward

provided there is no advantage to the non-offending team, a scrum will take place. The put-in will be performed by the half back of the non-offending team.

UNIT SKILLS OF NEW IMAGE RUGBY

The non-contact aspects of scrums and line-outs in New Image Rugby are a useful introduction to these units of the game. They provide the opportunity to establish correct techniques at an early age. The coach should be coaching the players in the fundamentals of throwing, jumping and catching in the line-out and body position in the scrum as outlined in this module.

BODY POSITION IN THE SCRUM

While pushing is not allowed by the laws of New Image Rugby correct body position will make the scrum more comfortable for the players.

The following are checklists for players that coaches should follow:

(1) Body Position
- (a) head up
- (b) back straight
- (c) shoulders above the hips
- (d) bend at the knees as well as the hips
- (e) have at least one arm bound around the body of a team-mate

(2) Props
- (a) bind on to the opposing prop with the free arm

(3) Locks
- (a) bind around the hips of the props with the outside arm

Note: All National Rugby Unions are continuously reviewing their Rules of Play, therefore for full details you are advised to contact direct the appropriate union.

RUGBY FOOTBALL UNION – Rugby Road, Twickenham, Middlesex, TW1 1DZ.

IRISH RUGBY FOOTBALL UNION – 62 Lansdowne Road, Dublin 4, Ireland.

SCOTTISH RUGBY UNION – Murrayfield, Edinbugh, EH12 5PJ

WELSH RUGBY UNION – Cardiff Arms Park, P.O.Box 22, Cardiff, CF1 1JL.

AUSTRALIAN RUGBY UNION – 353 Anzac Parade, Kingsford, New South Wales 2023, Australia. Postal Address: P.O. Box 333, Kingsford, New South Wales 2023.

NEW ZEALAND RUGBY FOOTBALL UNION – First Floor, Huddart Park Building, 1 Post Office Square, New Zealand. Postal Address: P.O. Box 2172, Wellington 1, New Zealand.